Jake Shimabukuro
LIVE IN JAPAN

Music transcriptions by Pete Billmann and Bill LaFleur

ISBN 978-1-4950-6115-8

HAL•LEONARD®
CORPORATION
7777 W. BLUEMOUND RD. P.O. BOX 13819 MILWAUKEE, WI 53213

For all works contained herein:
Unauthorized copying, arranging, adapting, recording, Internet posting, public performance,
or other distribution of the printed music in this publication is an infringement of copyright.
Infringers are liable under the law.

Visit Hal Leonard Online at
www.halleonard.com

CONTENTS

Medley: Trapped,
Me & Shirley T., Low Rider

Arranged by Jake Shimabukuro

A

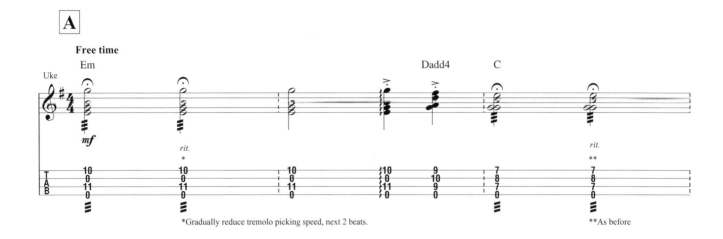

*Gradually reduce tremolo picking speed, next 2 beats.   **As before

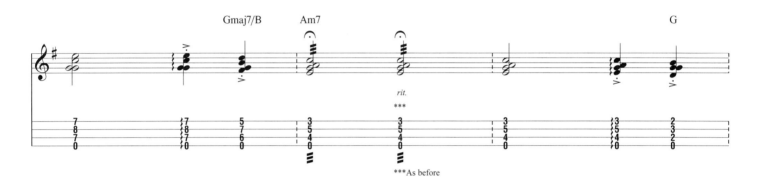

***As before

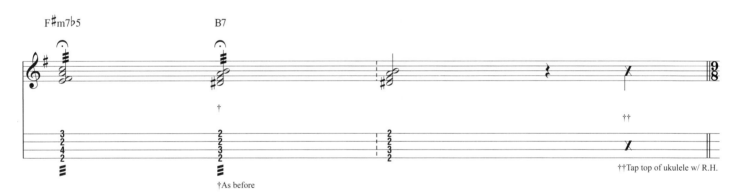

†As before   ††Tap top of ukulele w/ R.H.

B

TRAPPED 2010
Written by Jake Shimabukuro

Moderately fast ♩. = 147

†††Em

†††Chord symbols reflect basic harmony.

TRAPPED 2010
Copyright © 2010 Uke Ox Publishing (BMI)
Courtesy of Hitchhike Records
All Rights Reserved   Used by Permission

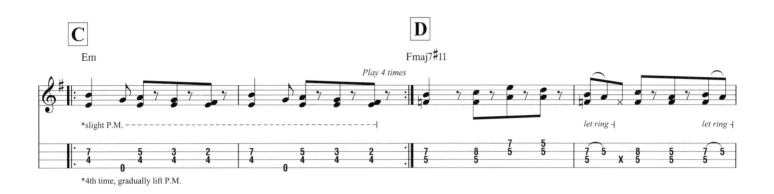

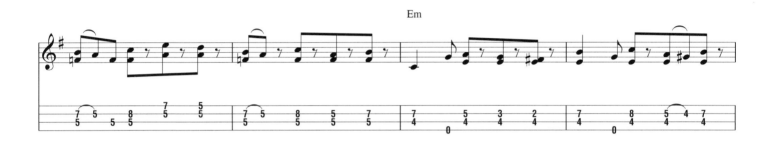

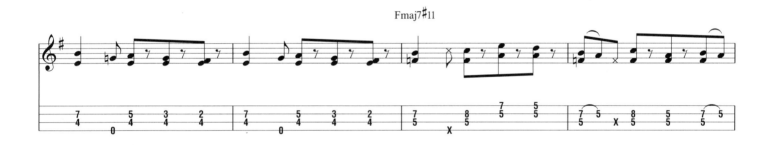

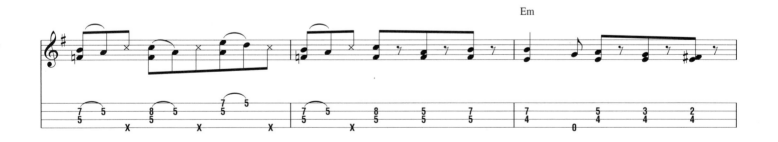

E

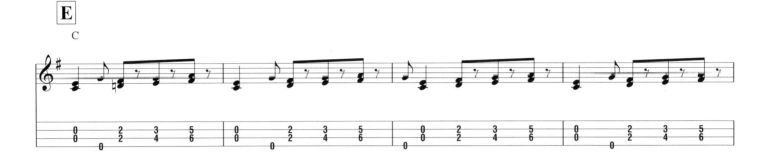

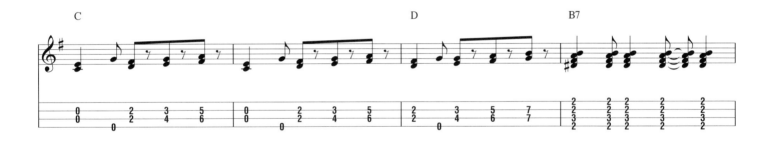

F

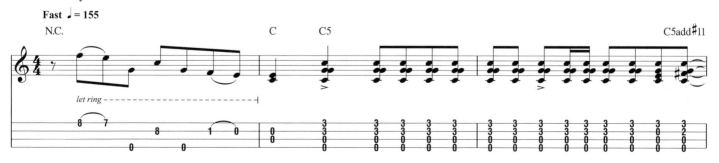

ME & SHIRLEY T.
Copyright © 2004 Uke Ox Publishing
All Rights Administered by Sony/ATV Music Publishing LLC, 424 Church Street, Suite 1200, Nashville, TN 37219
International Copyright Secured   All Rights Reserved

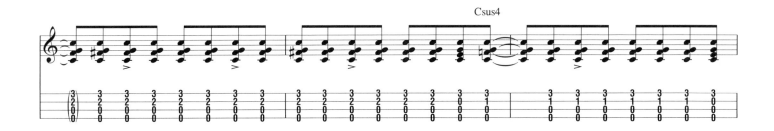

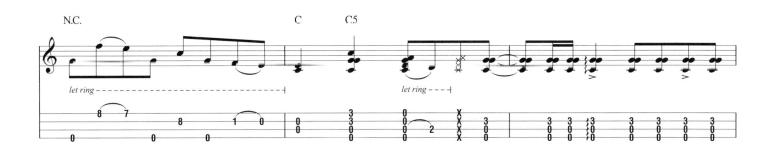

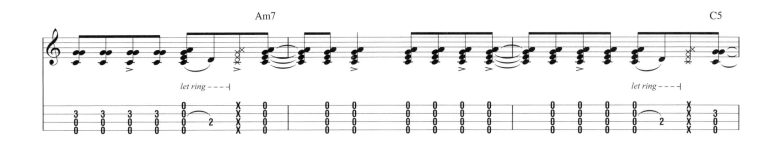

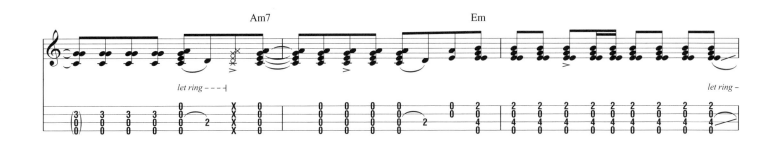

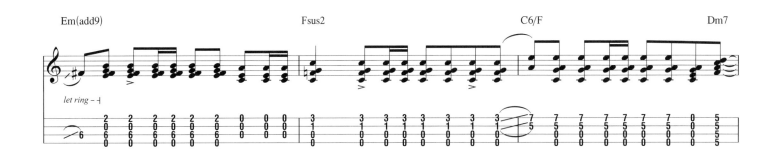

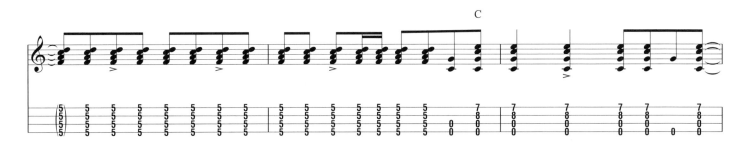

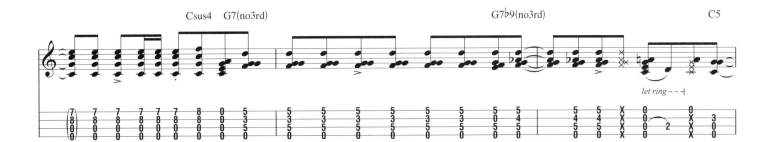

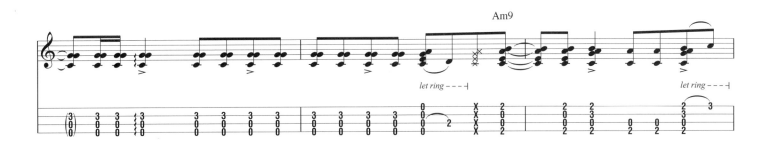

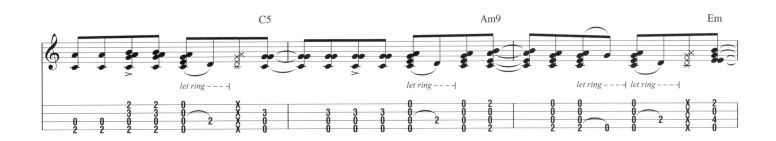

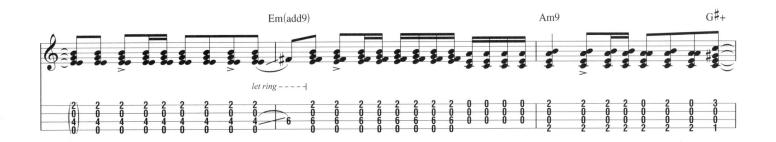

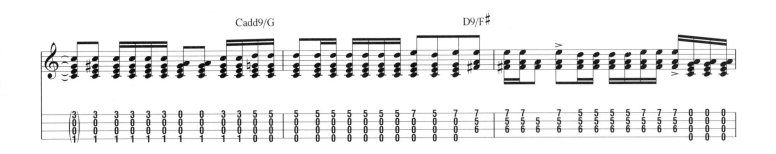

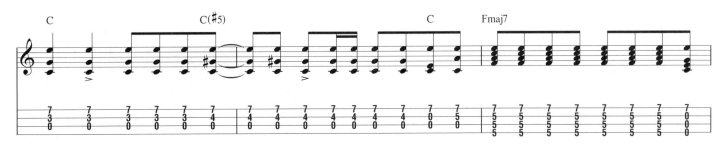

L

1., 2., 3.   4.

LOW RIDER
Words and Music by Sylvester Allen, Harold R. Brown,
Morris Dickerson, Jerry Goldstein, Leroy Jordan,
Lee Oskar, Charles W. Miller and Howard Scott

Fast ♩ = 150

N.C.

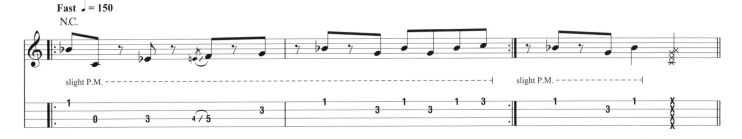

M

C7

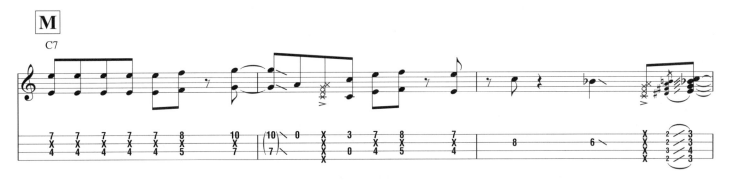

LOW RIDER
Copyright © 1975 Far Out Music, Inc.
Copyright Renewed
This arrangement Copyright © 2015 Far Out Music, Inc.
All Rights Administered by BMG Rights Management (US) LLC
All Rights Reserved   Used by Permission

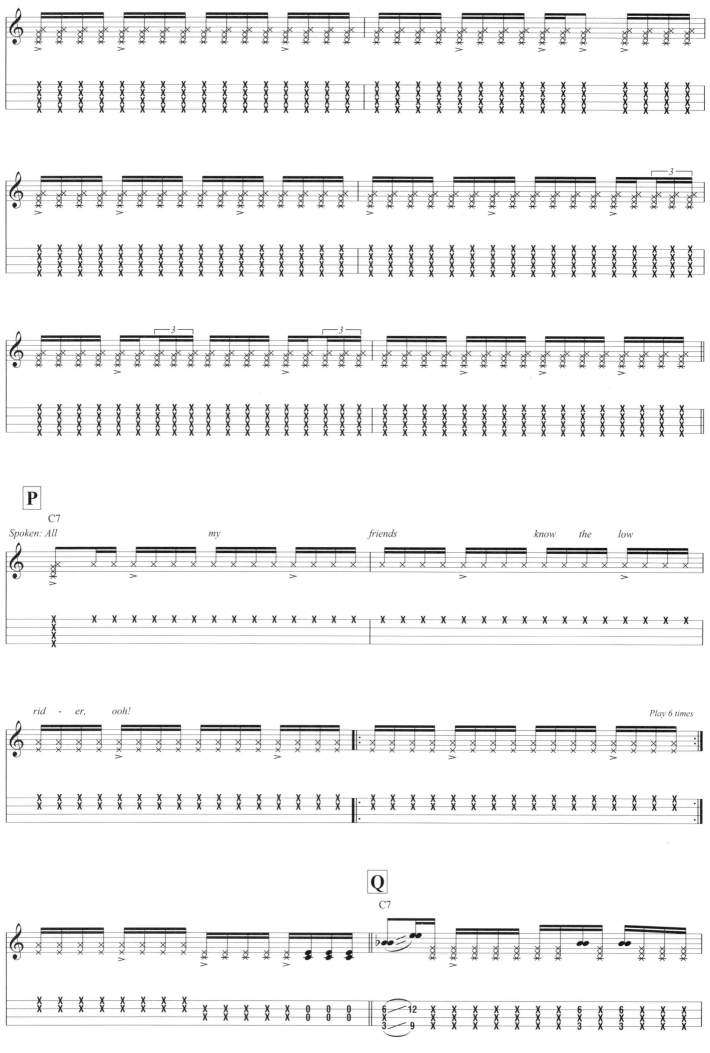

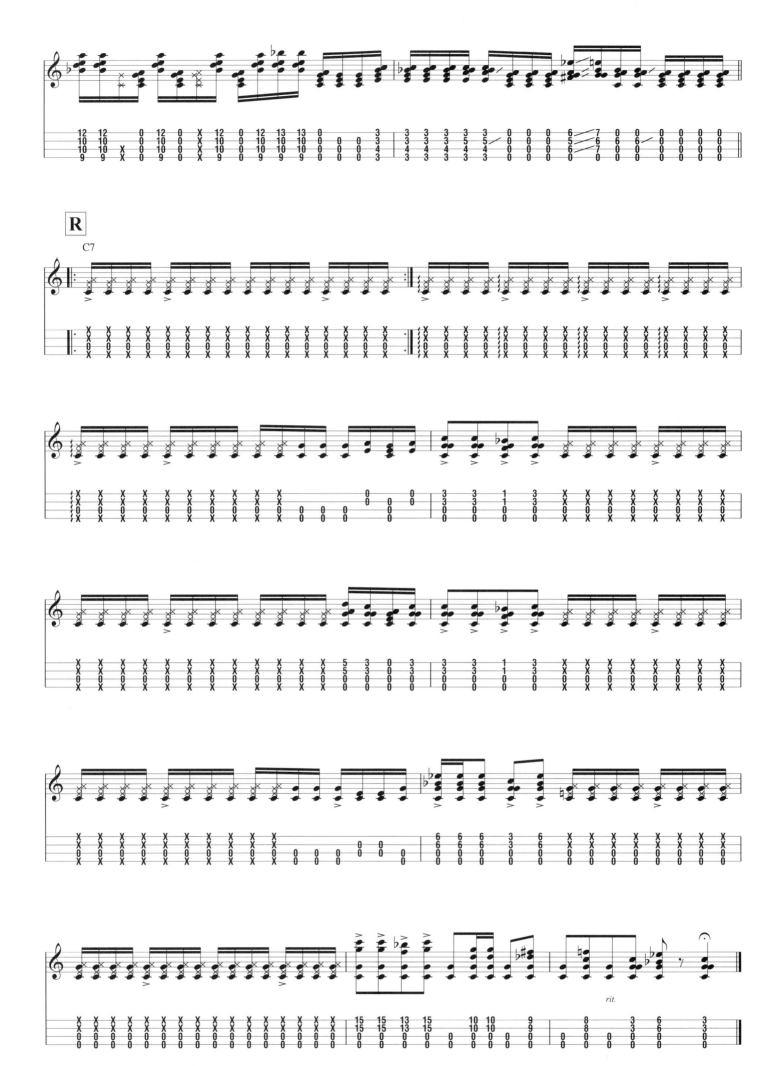

Passport

Written by Jake Shimabukuro and Dean K. Taba

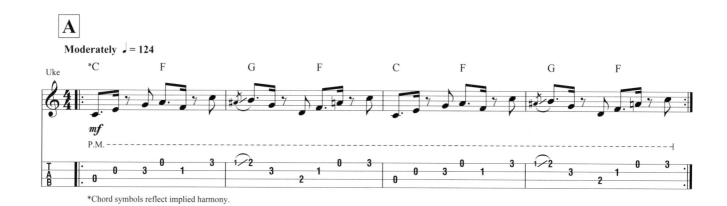

*Chord symbols reflect implied harmony.

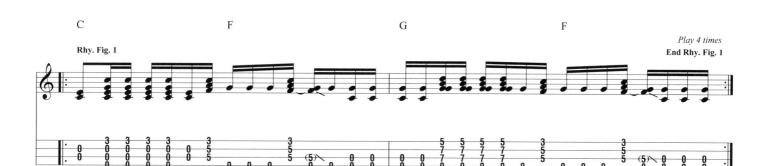

*Loop pedal regeneration

Copyright © 2015 Uke Ox Publishing (BMI) and Disk Eye Music (ASCAP)
All Rights Reserved   Used by Permission

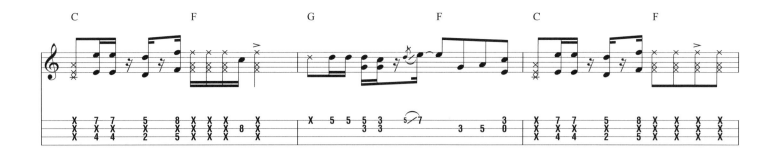

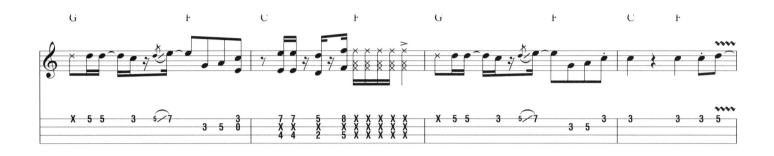

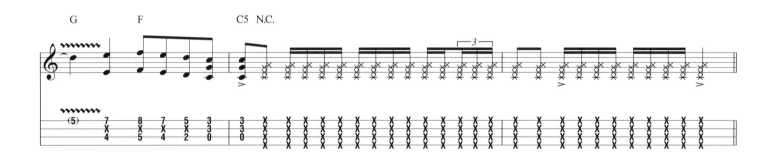

C

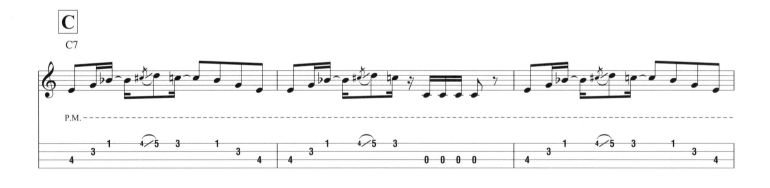

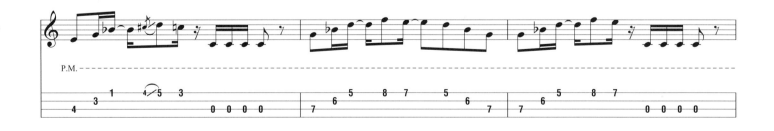

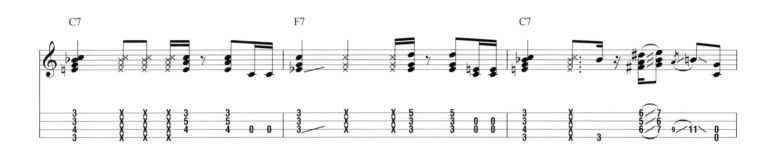

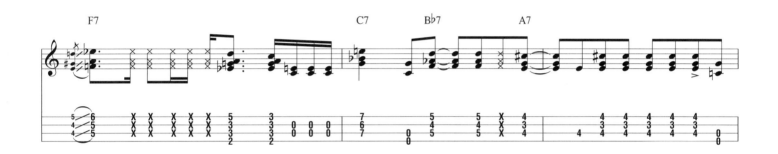

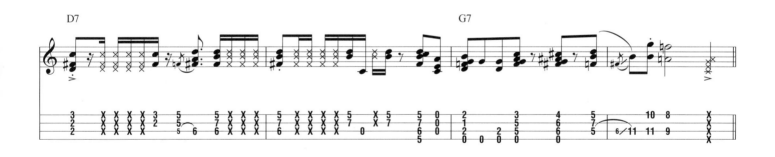

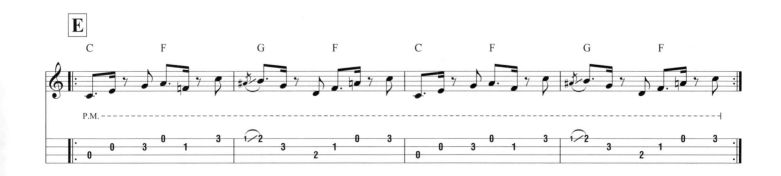

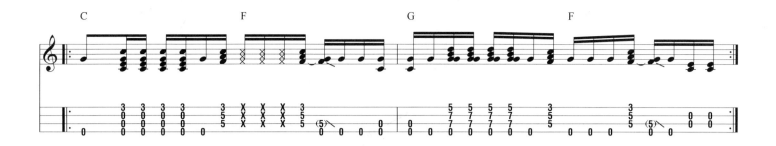

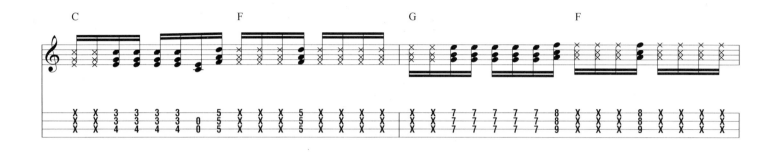

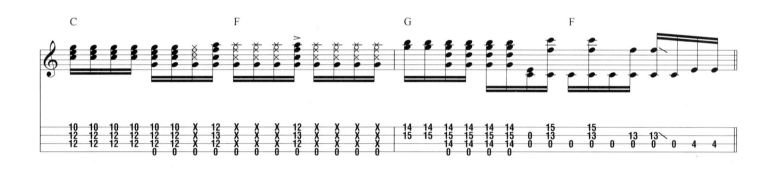

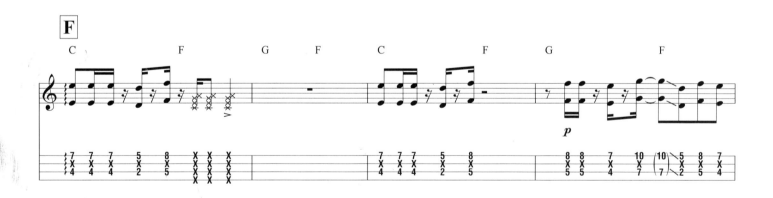

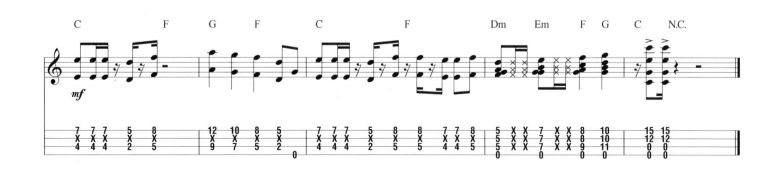

Red-Eye

Written by Jake Shimabukuro

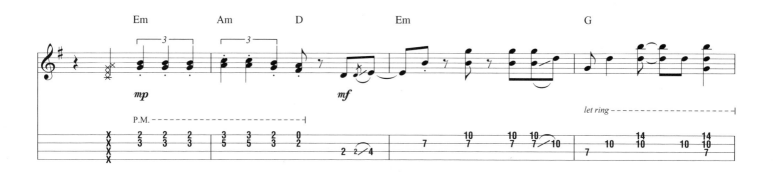

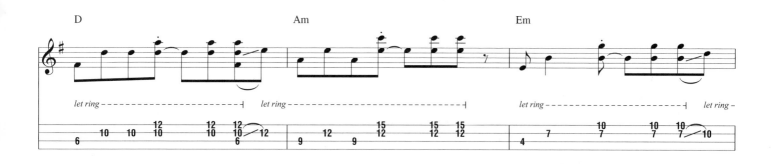

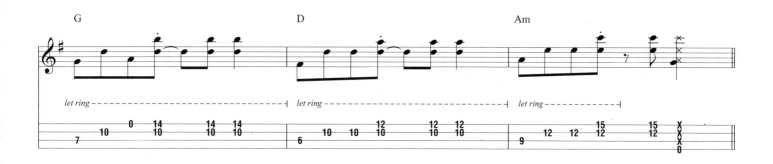

Copyright © 2015 Uke Ox Publishing (BMI)
All Rights Reserved   Used by Permission

B

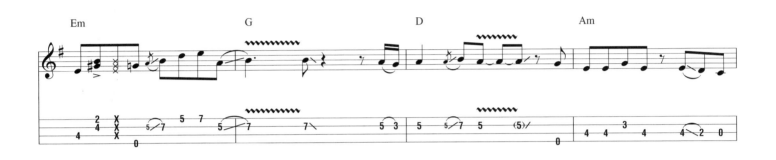

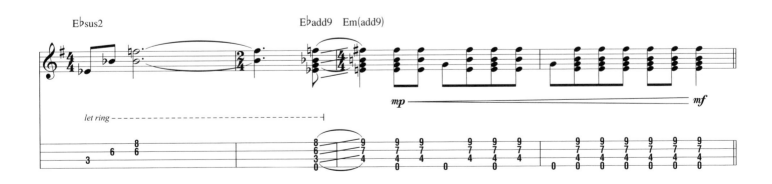

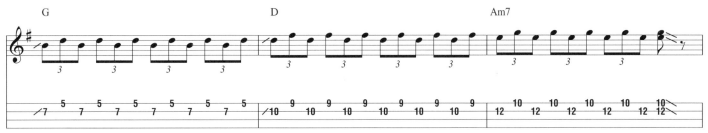

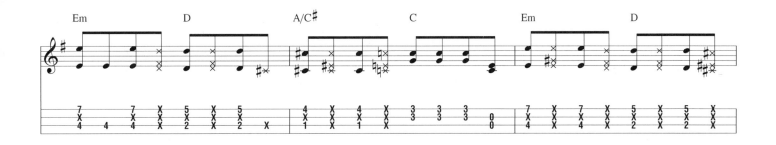

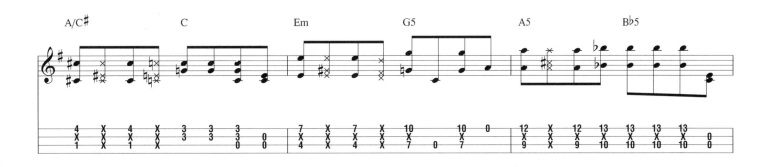

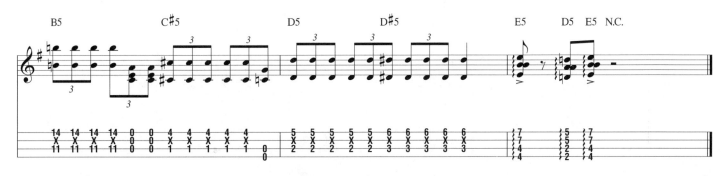

Ichigo Ichie

Written by Jake Shimabukuro

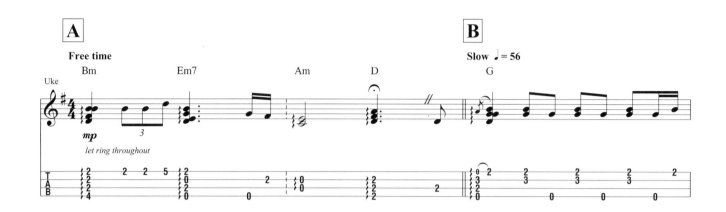

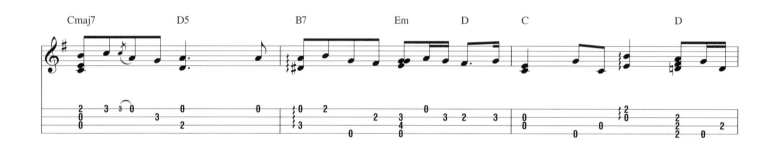

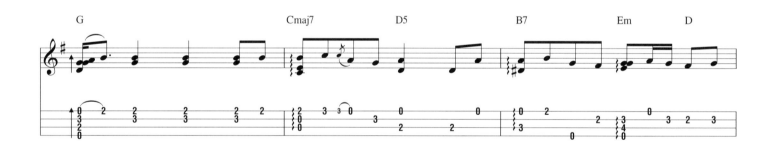

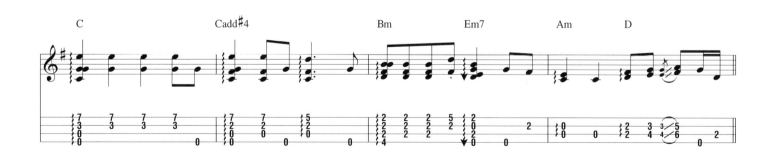

Copyright © 2008 Uke Ox Publishing (BMI)
All Rights Reserved   Used by Permission

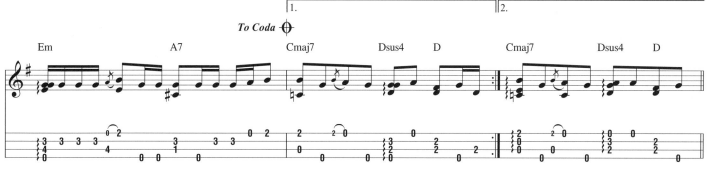

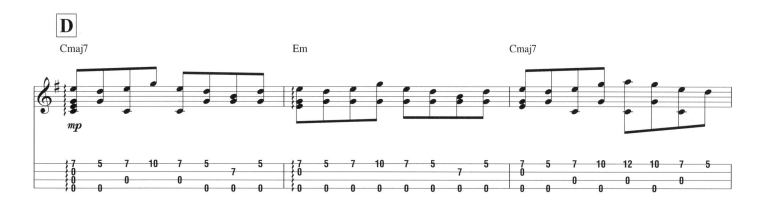

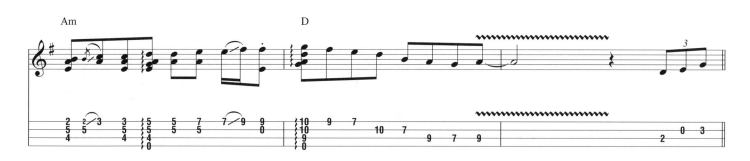

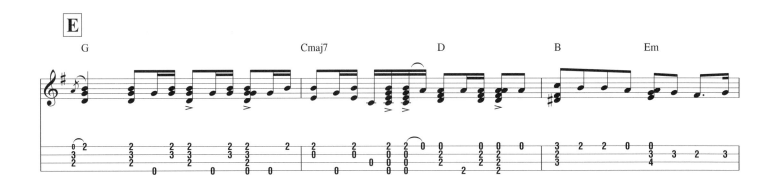

D.S. al Coda
(take 1st ending)

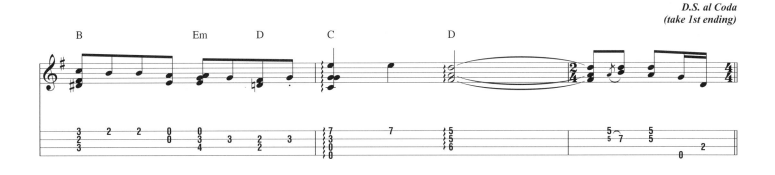

Coda

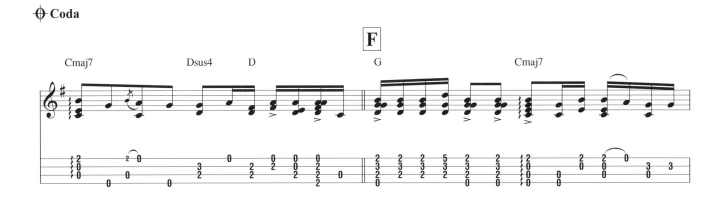

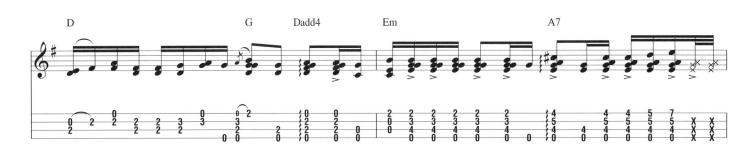

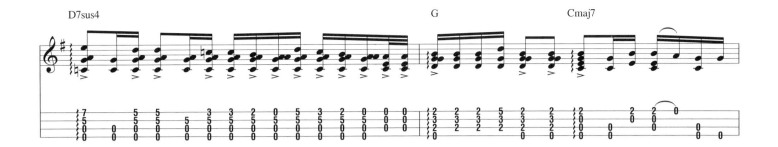

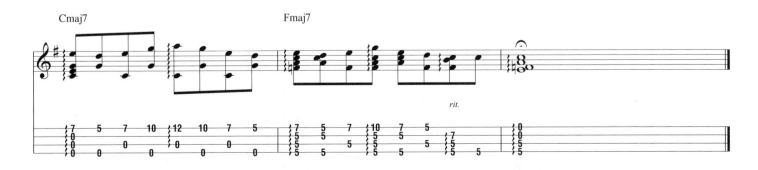

I'll Be There

Words and Music by Berry Gordy, Hal Davis, Willie Hutch and Bob West

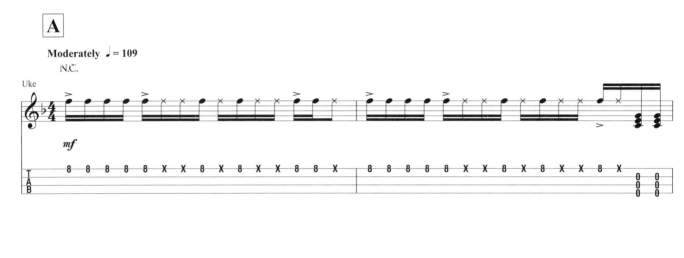

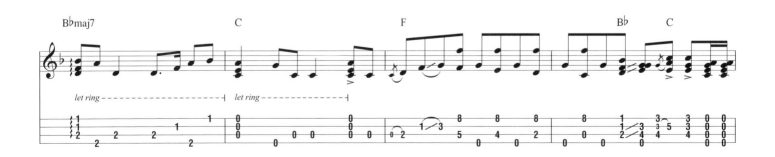

© 1970, 1975 (Renewed 1998, 2003) JOBETE MUSIC CO., INC.
All Rights Controlled and Administered by EMI APRIL MUSIC INC.
All Rights Reserved   International Copyright Secured   Used by Permission

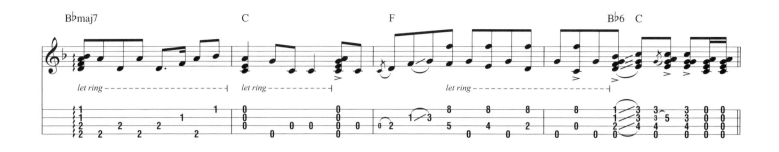

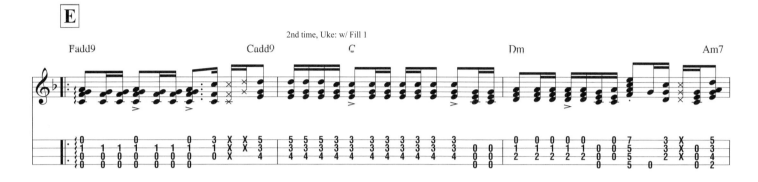

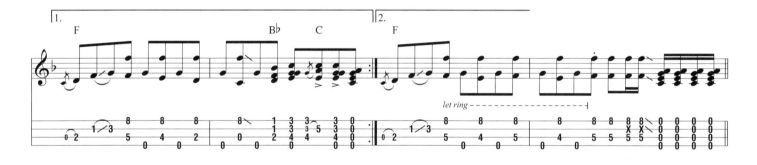

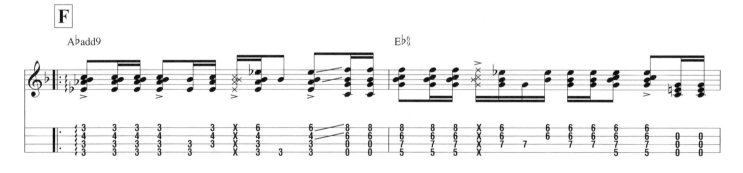

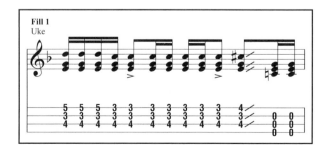

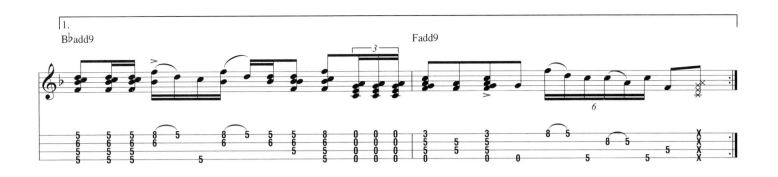

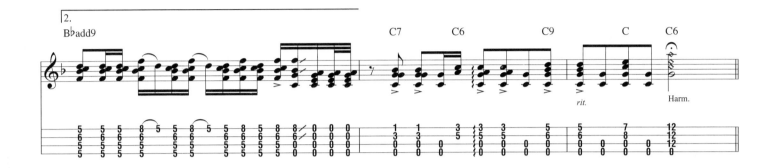

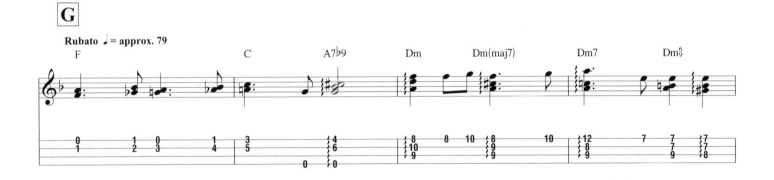

Oama

Written by Jake Shimabukuro

*Chord symbols reflect overall harmony.

Copyright © 2015 Uke Ox Publishing (BMI)
All Rights Reserved   Used by Permission

D.S. al Coda 2
(take repeat)

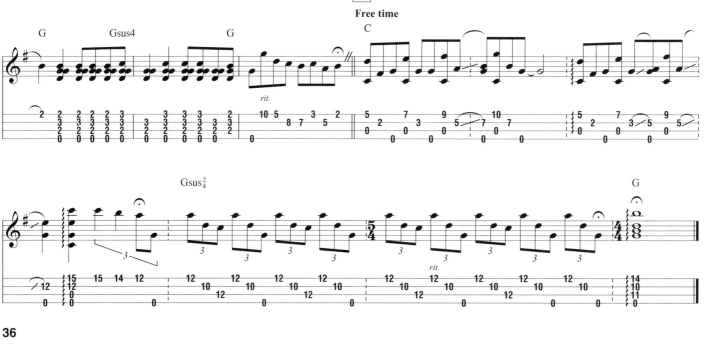

Travels

Written by Jake Shimabukuro

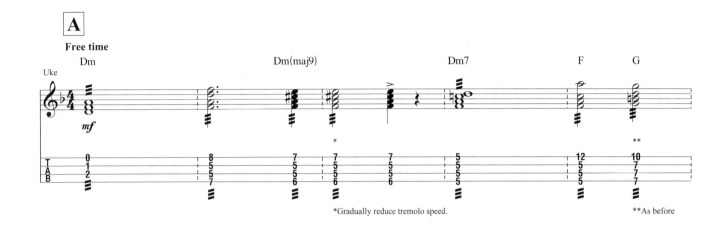

*Gradually reduce tremolo speed.

**As before

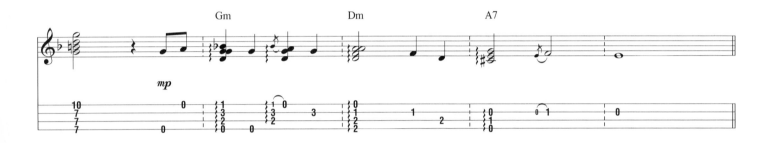

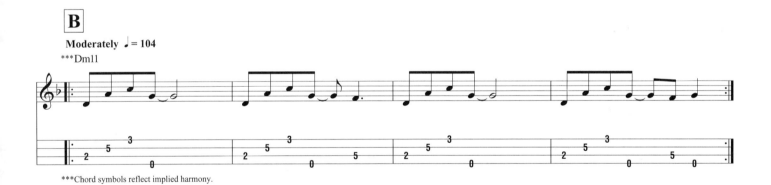

***Chord symbols reflect implied harmony.

Copyright © 2015 Uke Ox Publishing (BMI)
All Rights Reserved   Used by Permission

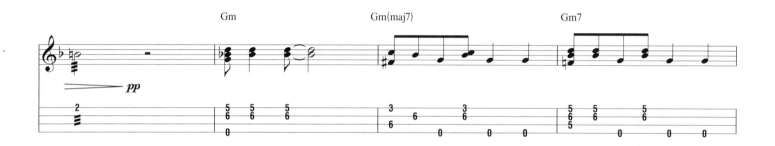

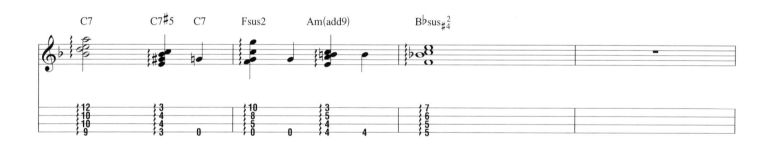

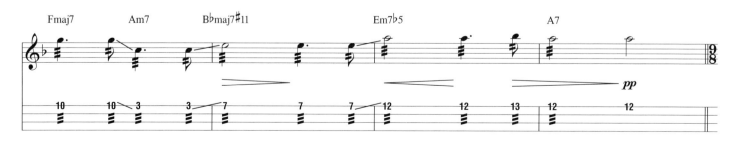

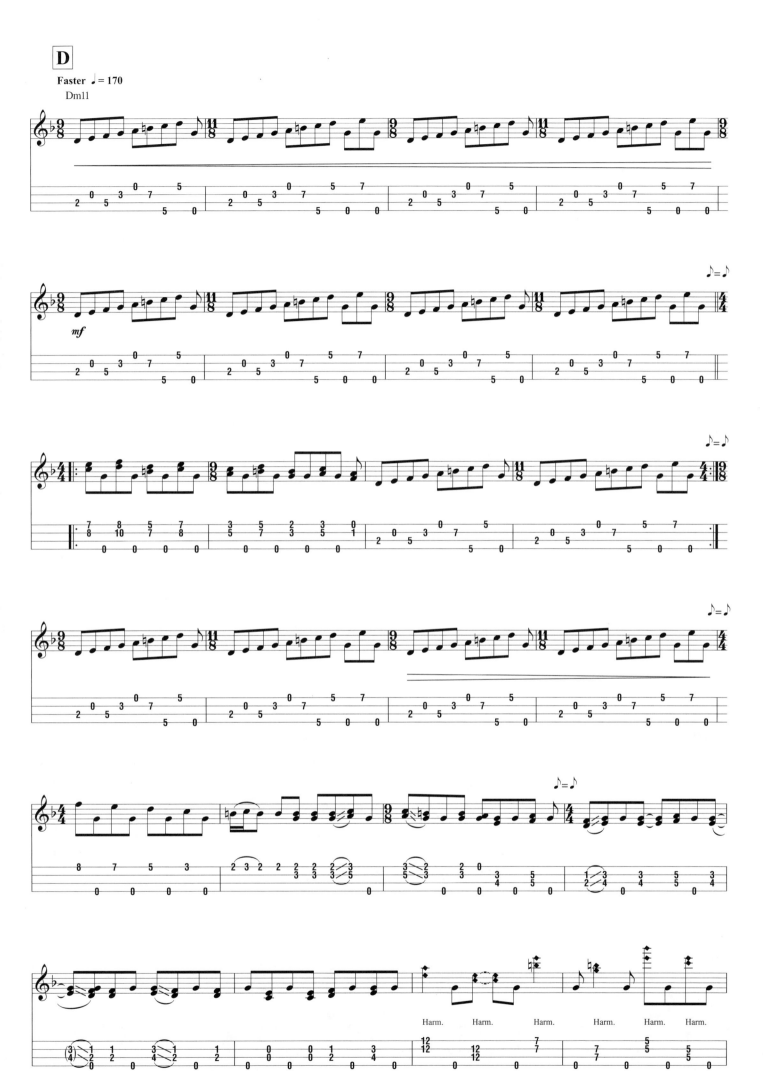

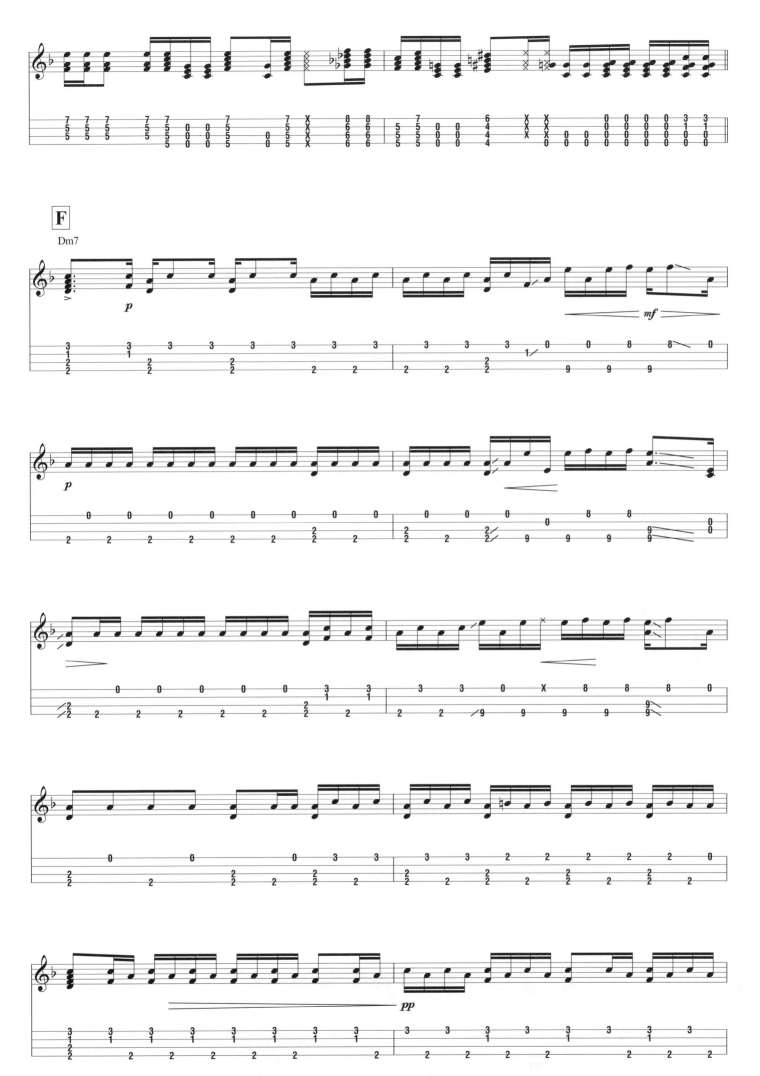

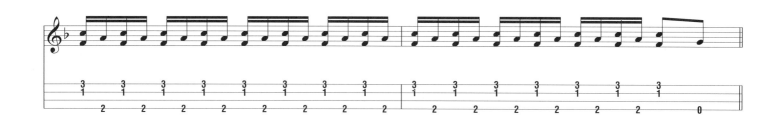

G

Dm11

Play 3 times

Kawika

Traditional Hawaiian Song
Arranged by Jake Shimabukuro

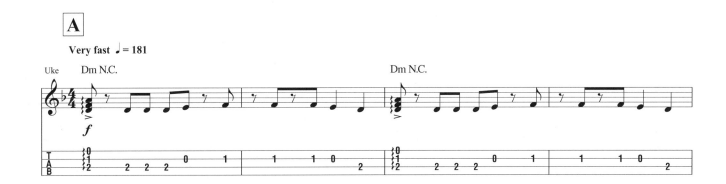

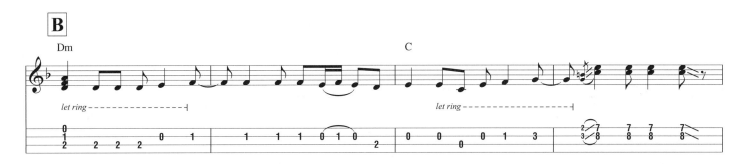

Copyright © 2015 Uke Ox Publishing (BMI)
All Rights Reserved   Used by Permission

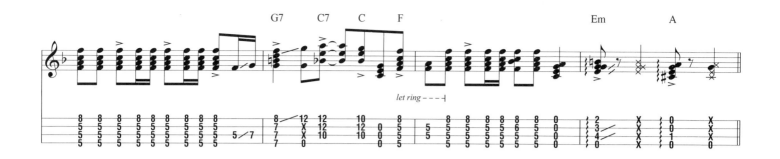

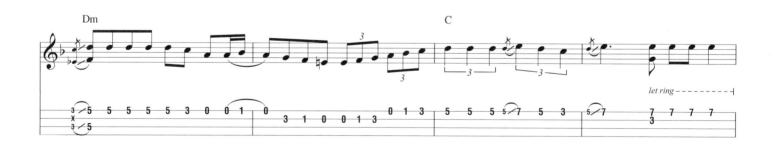

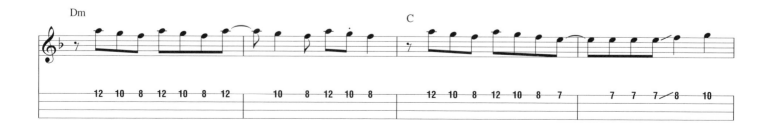

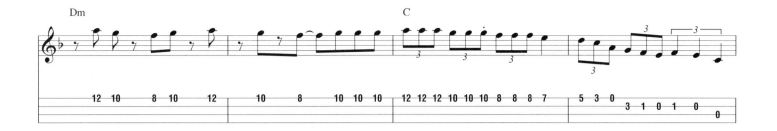
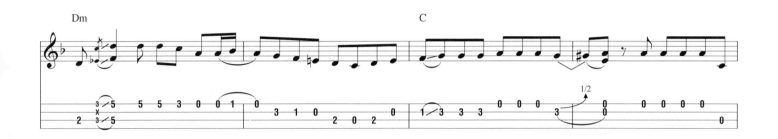
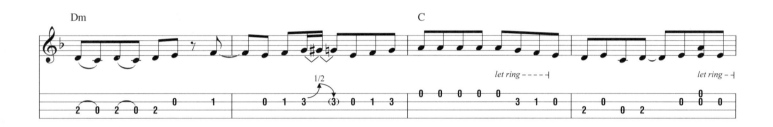
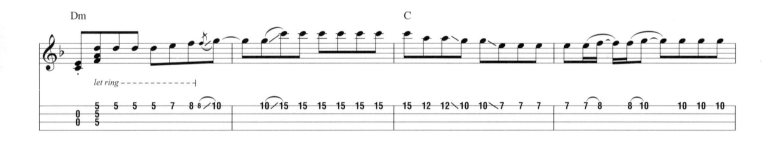
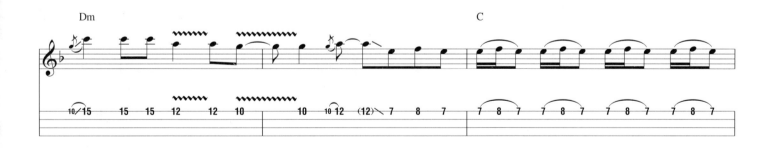
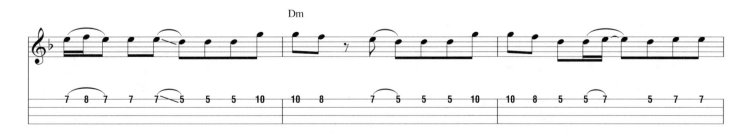

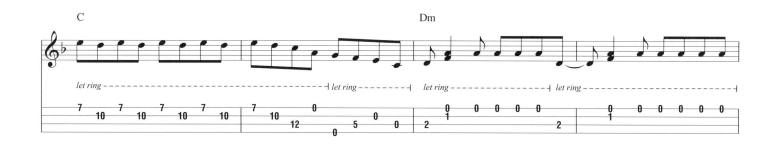

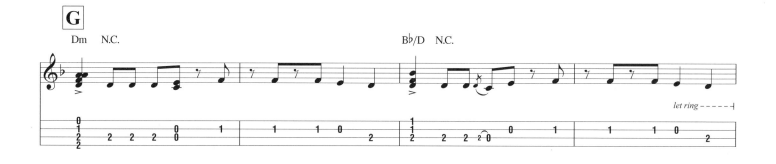

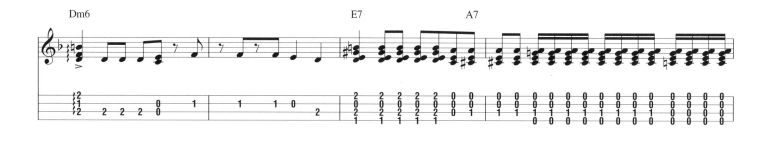

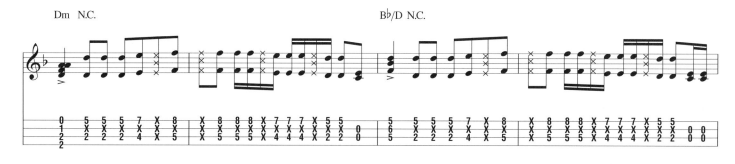

Hula Girl

Written by Jake Shimabukuro

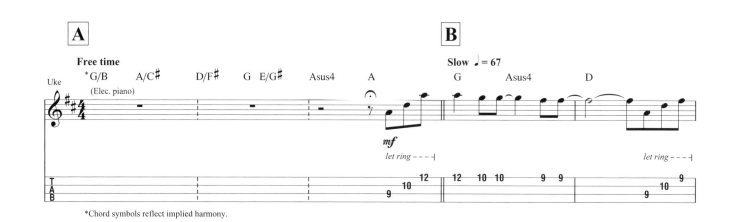

*Chord symbols reflect implied harmony.

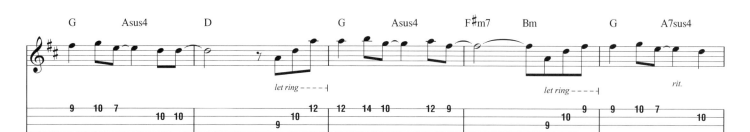

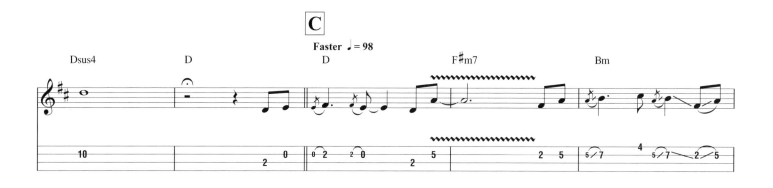

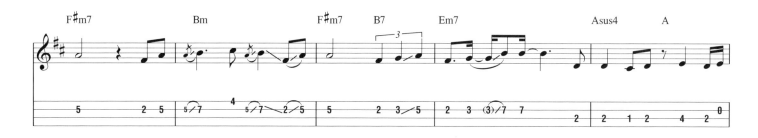

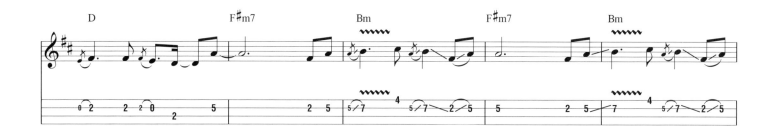

Copyright © 2007 Uke Ox Publishing
All Rights Administered by Sony/ATV Music Publishing LLC, 424 Church Street, Suite 1200, Nashville, TN 37219
International Copyright Secured   All Rights Reserved

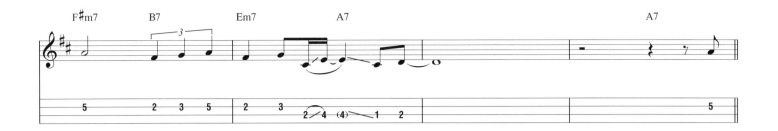

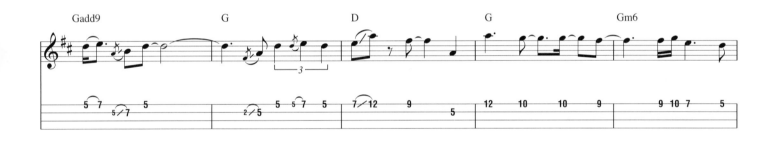

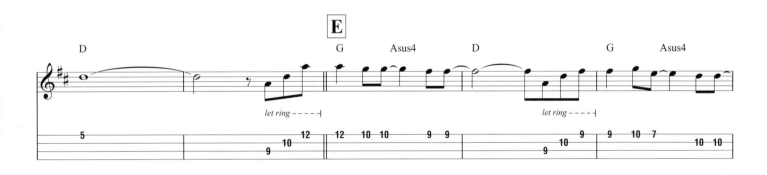

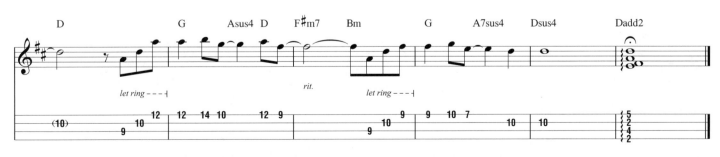

Blue Roses Falling

Written by Jake Shimabukuro

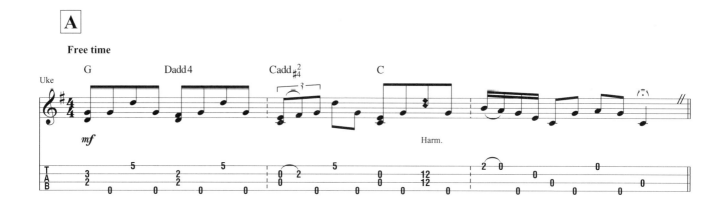

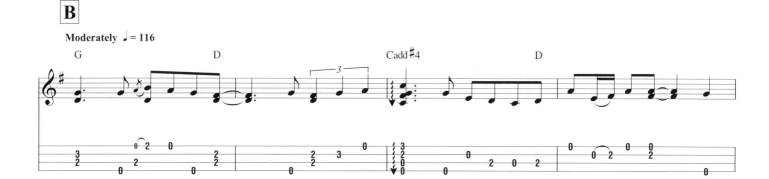

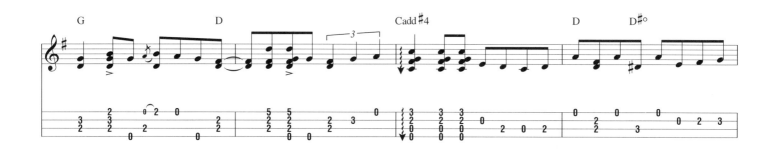

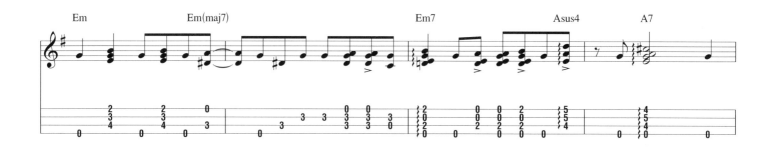

Copyright © 2004 Uke Ox Publishing
All Rights Administered by Sony/ATV Music Publishing LLC, 424 Church Street, Suite 1200, Nashville, TN 37219
International Copyright Secured   All Rights Reserved

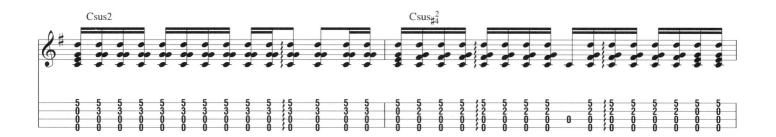

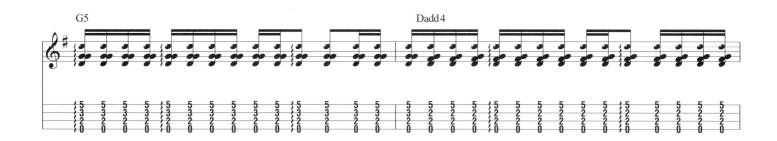

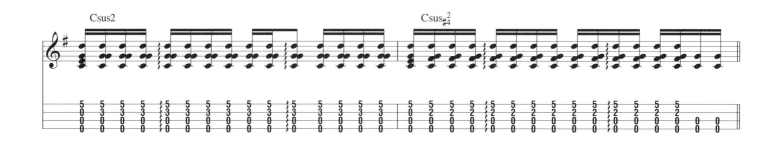

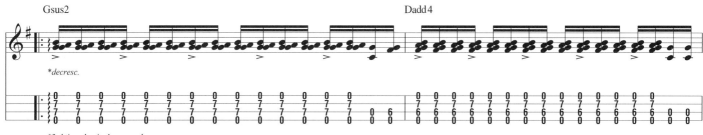

*decresc.

*3rd time, begin decrescendo.

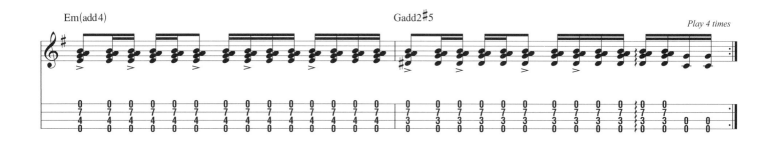

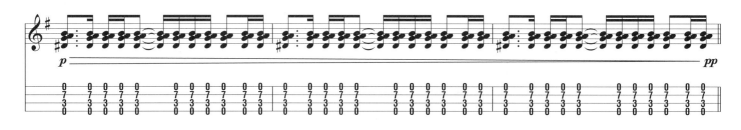

Bohemian Rhapsody

Words and Music by Freddie Mercury

Copyright © 1975 Queen Music Ltd.
Copyright Renewed
All Rights Administered by Sony/ATV Music Publishing LLC, 424 Church Street, Suite 1200, Nashville, TN 37219
International Copyright Secured   All Rights Reserved

*Harp harmonics produced by lightly touching
12 frets above fretted note while picking string.

**Chord symbols reflect overall harmony.

Dragon

Written by Jake Shimabukuro

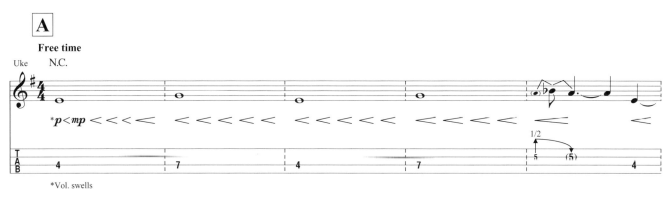

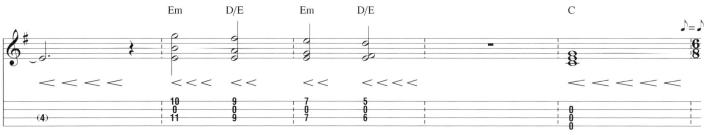

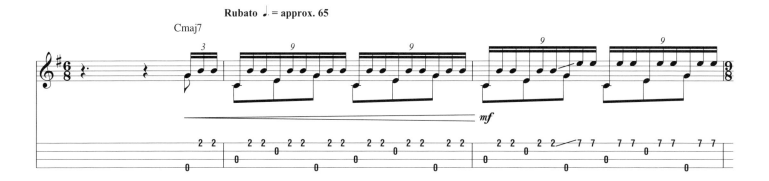

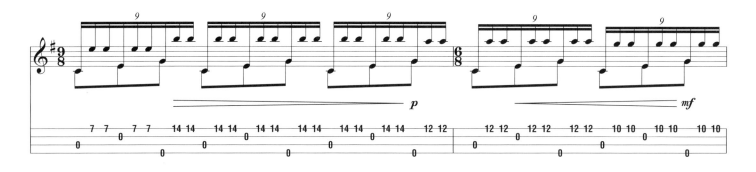

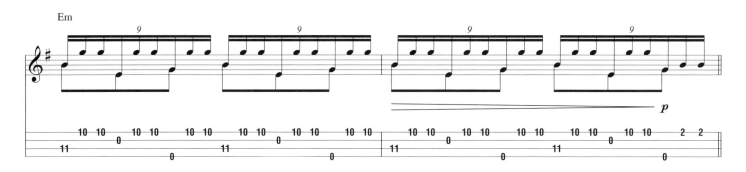

Copyright © 2004 Uke Ox Publishing
All Rights Administered by Sony/ATV Music Publishing LLC, 424 Church Street, Suite 1200, Nashville, TN 37219
International Copyright Secured   All Rights Reserved

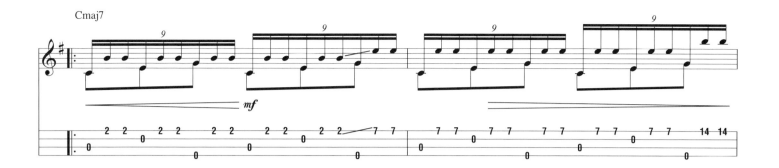
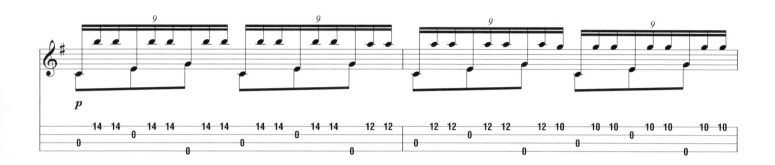
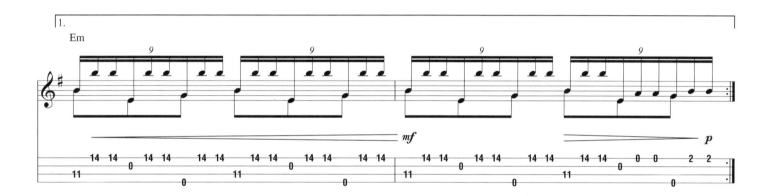
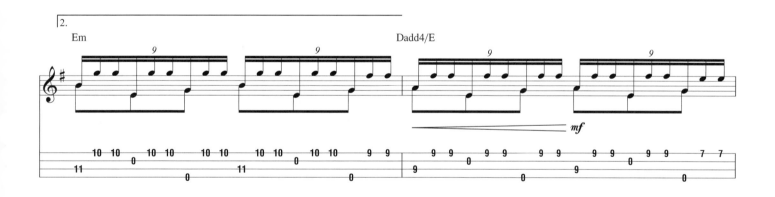
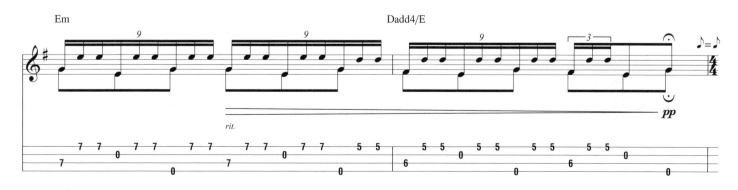

Free time

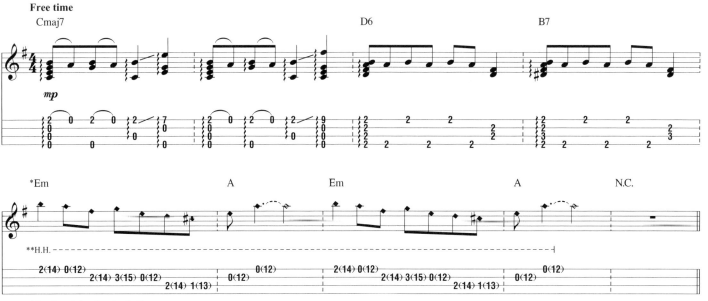

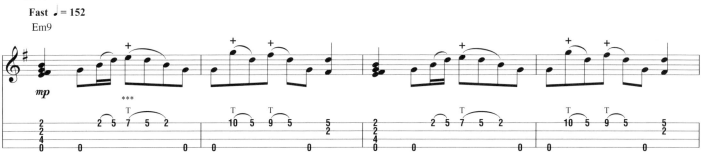

*Chord symbols reflect implied harmony.

**Harp Harm.: Lightly touch string at fret number in parentheses w/
pick-hand index finger while simultaneously picking fretted or open note.

B

Fast ♩ = 152

***Tapping: Hammer ("tap") the fret indicated w/ pick-hand
index finger and pull off to the next note fretted by the fret hand.

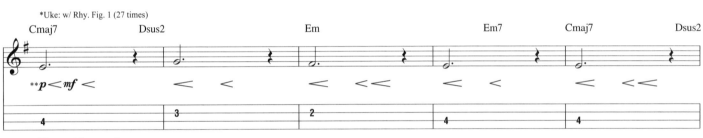

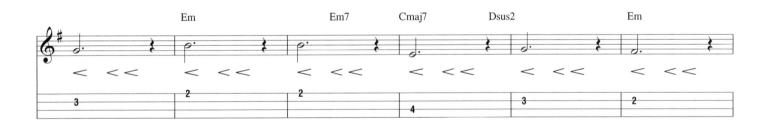

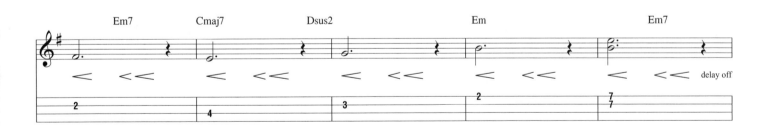

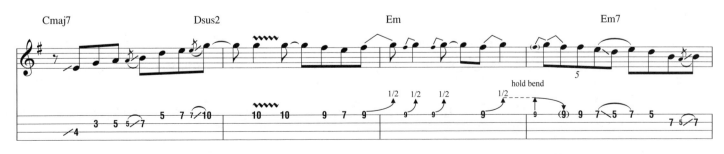

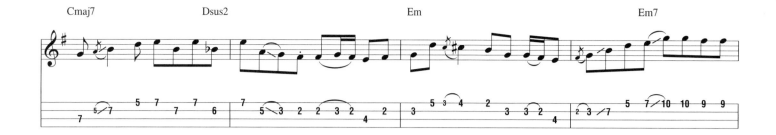

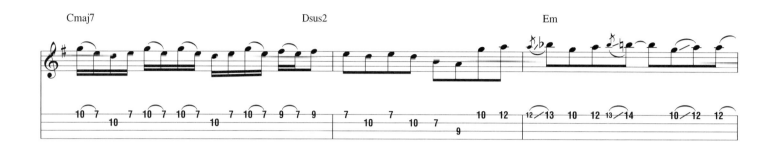

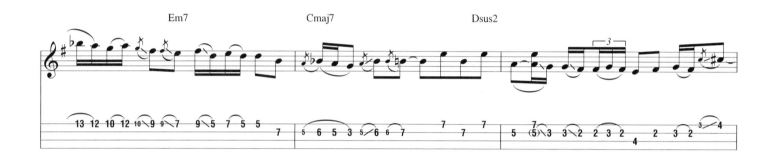

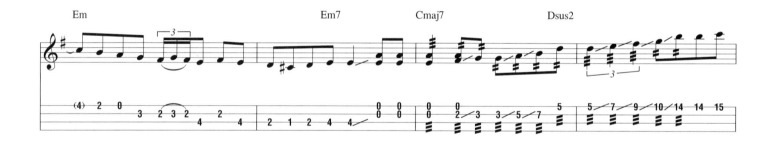

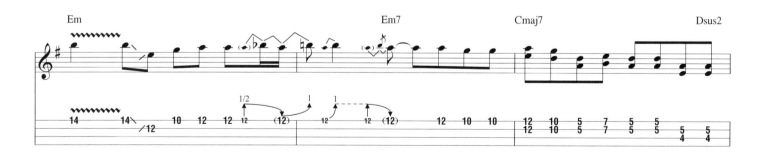

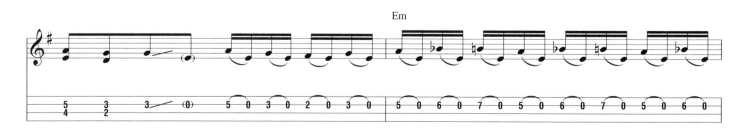

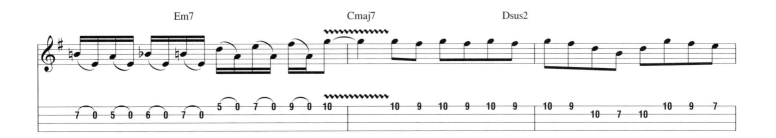

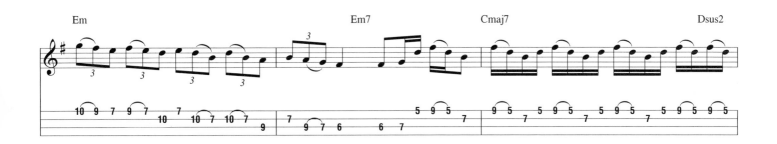

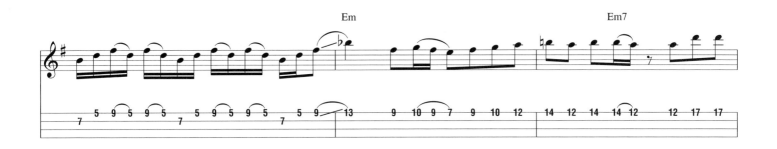

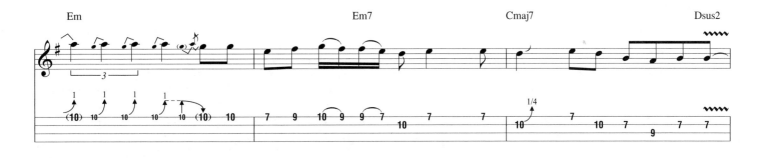

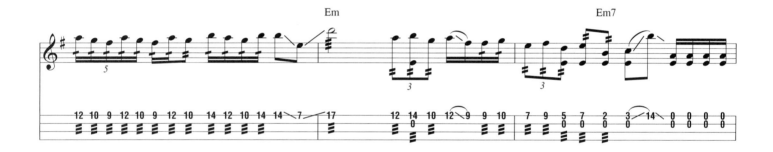

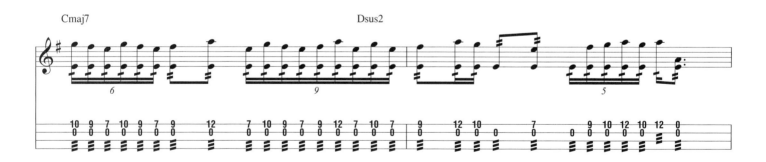

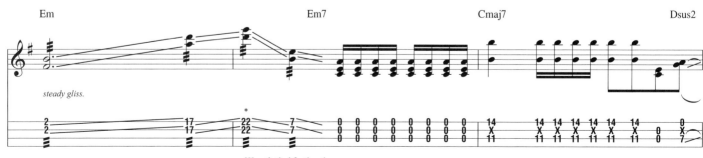

*Hypothetical fret location.

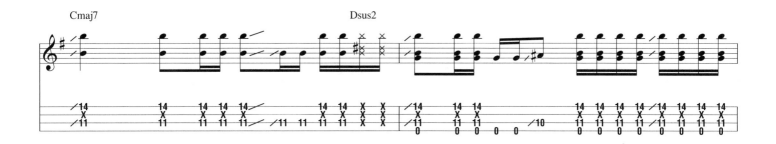

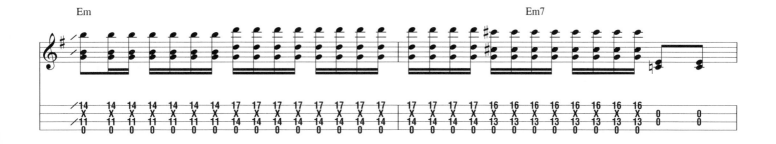

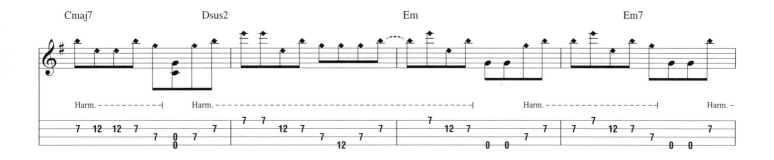

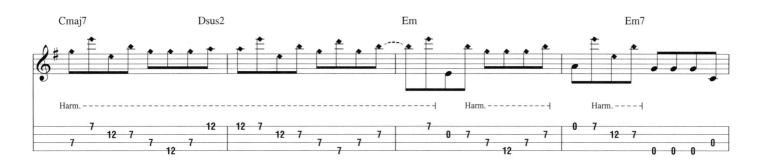

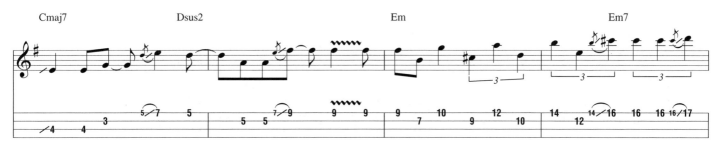

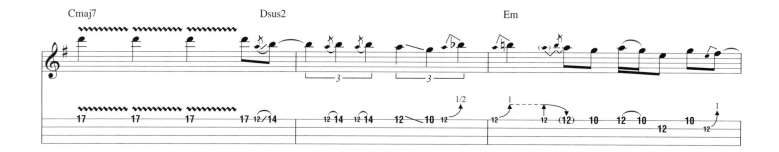

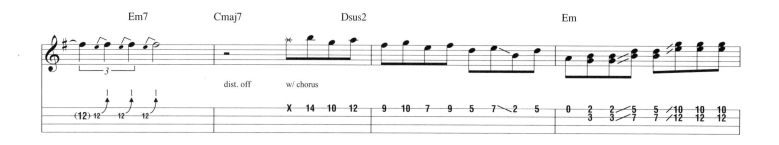

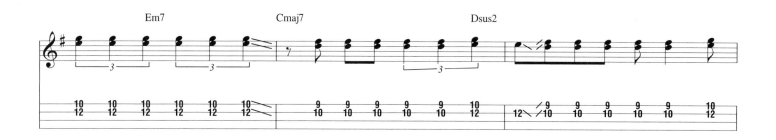

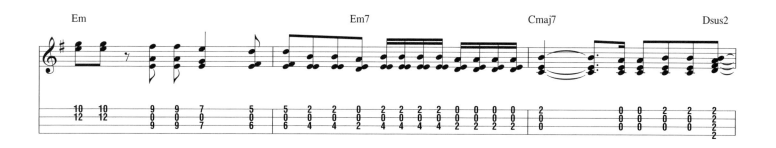

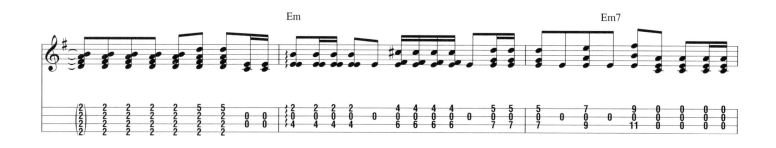

3rd Stream

Written by Jake Shimabukuro

Copyright © 2004 Uke Ox Publishing
All Rights Administered by Sony/ATV Music Publishing LLC, 424 Church Street, Suite 1200, Nashville, TN 37219
International Copyright Secured   All Rights Reserved

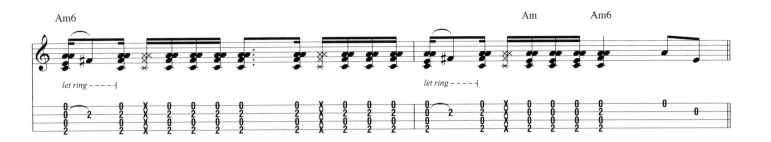

B

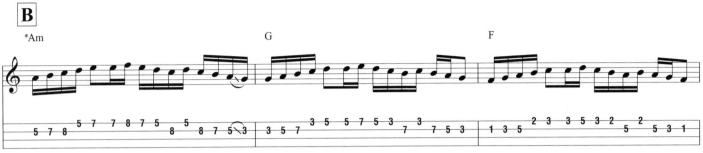

*Chord symbols reflect overall harmony.

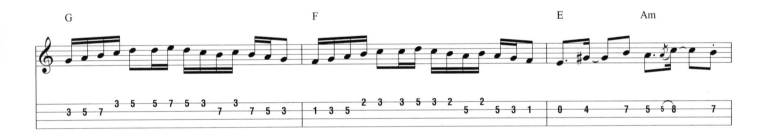

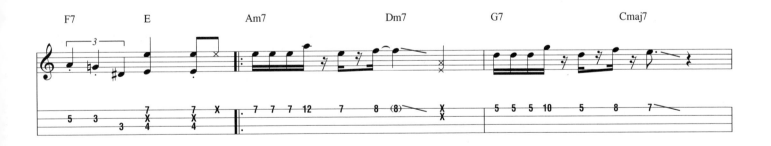

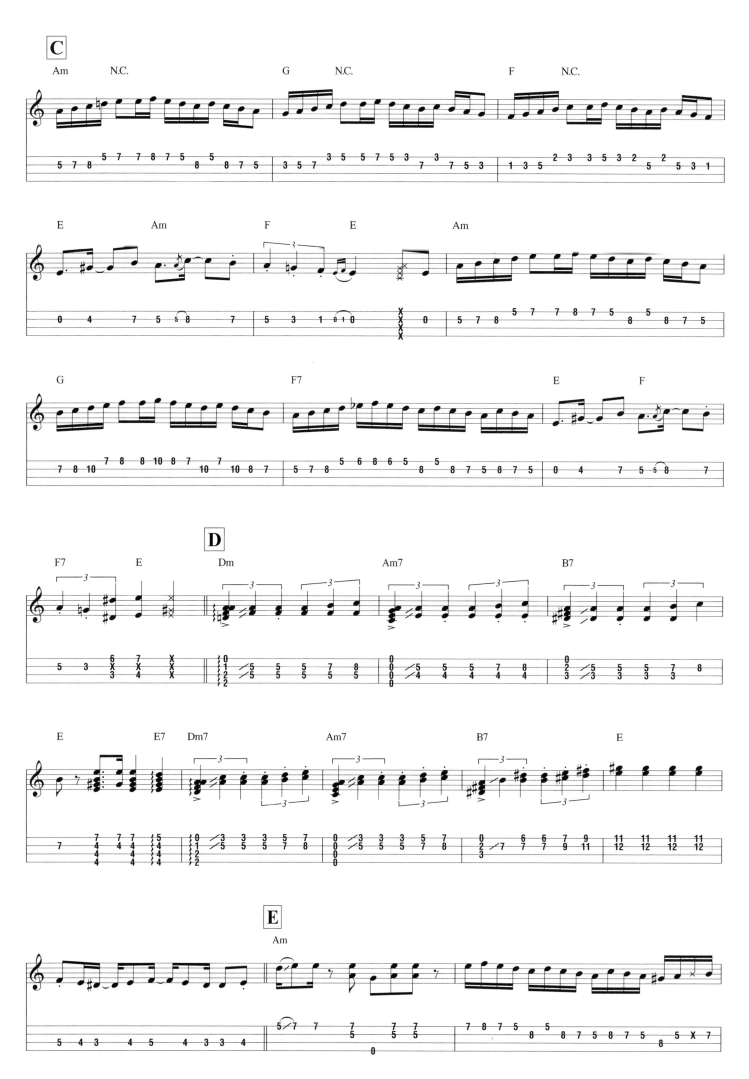

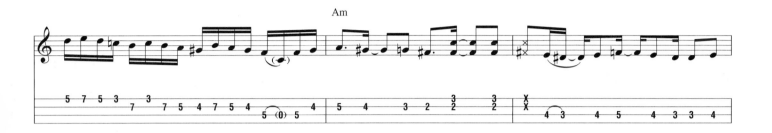

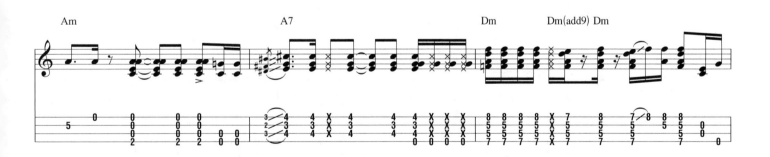

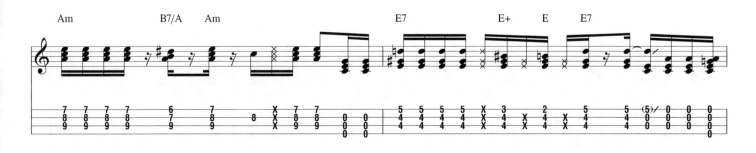

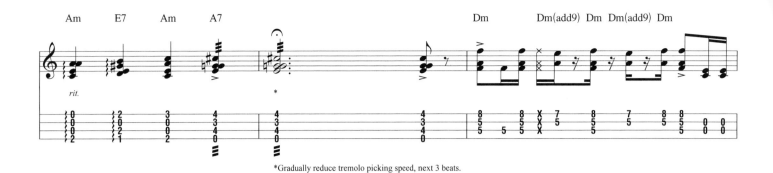

*Gradually reduce tremolo picking speed, next 3 beats.

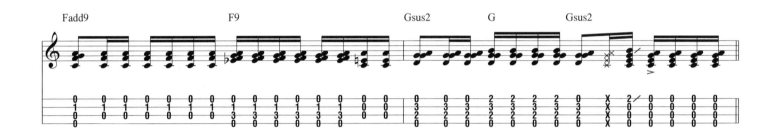

F

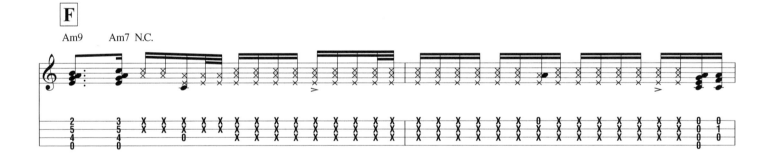

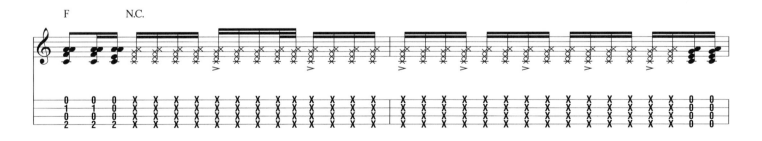

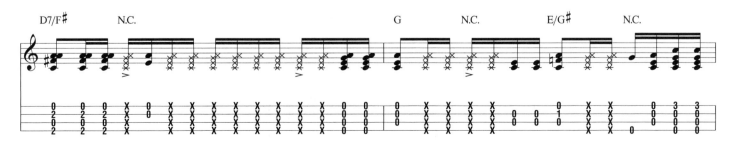

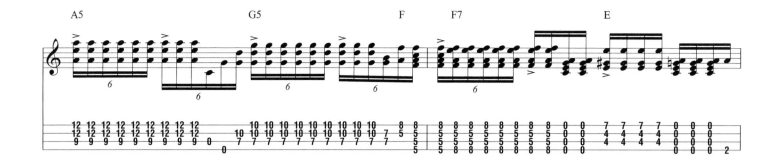

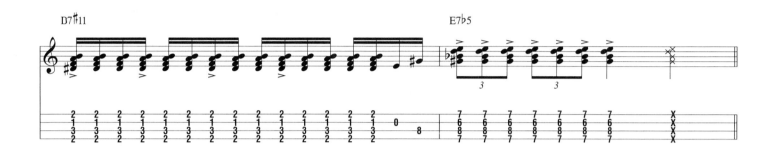

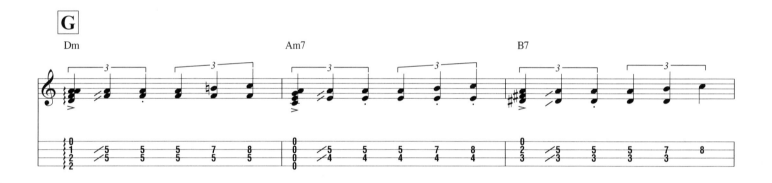

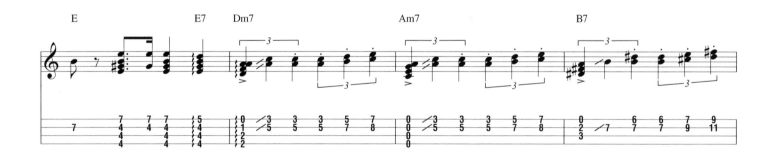

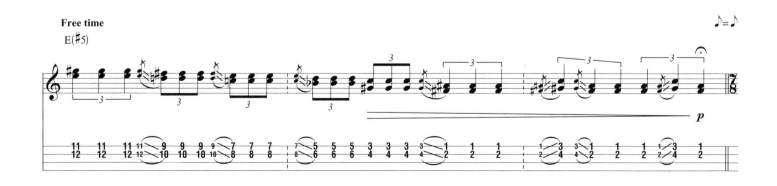

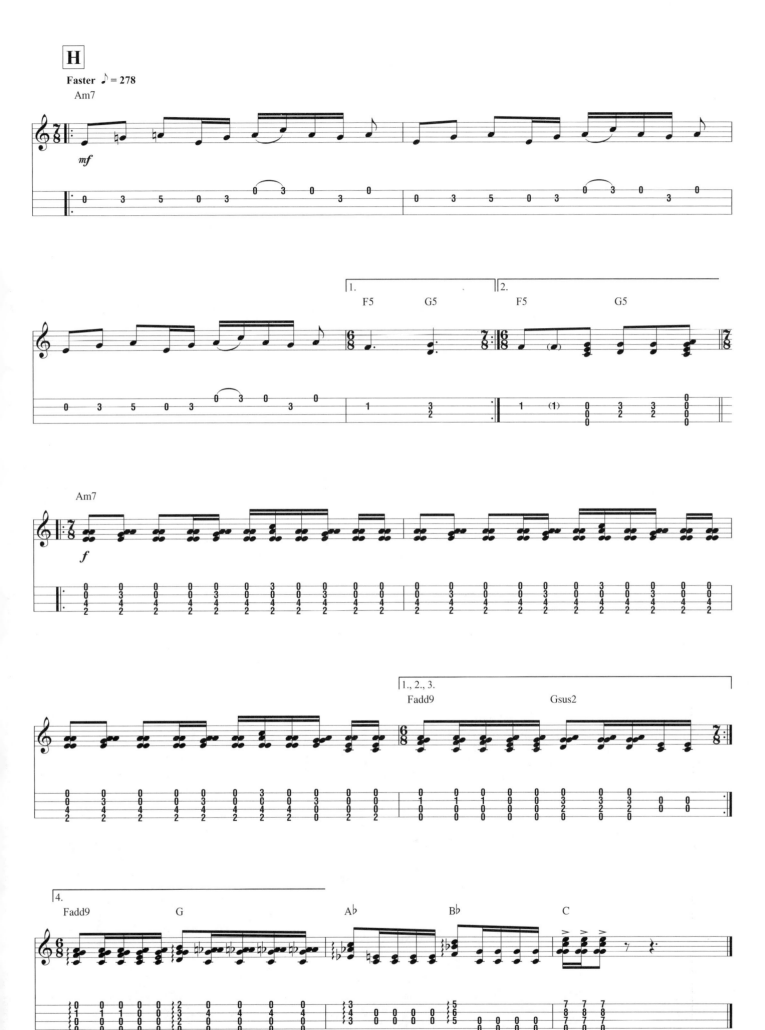

Orange World

Written by Jake Shimabukuro

*Chord symbols reflect implied harmony.

Copyright © 2004 Uke Ox Publishing
All Rights Administered by Sony/ATV Music Publishing LLC, 424 Church Street, Suite 1200, Nashville, TN 37219
International Copyright Secured   All Rights Reserved

*Tap top of ukulele w/ R.H.

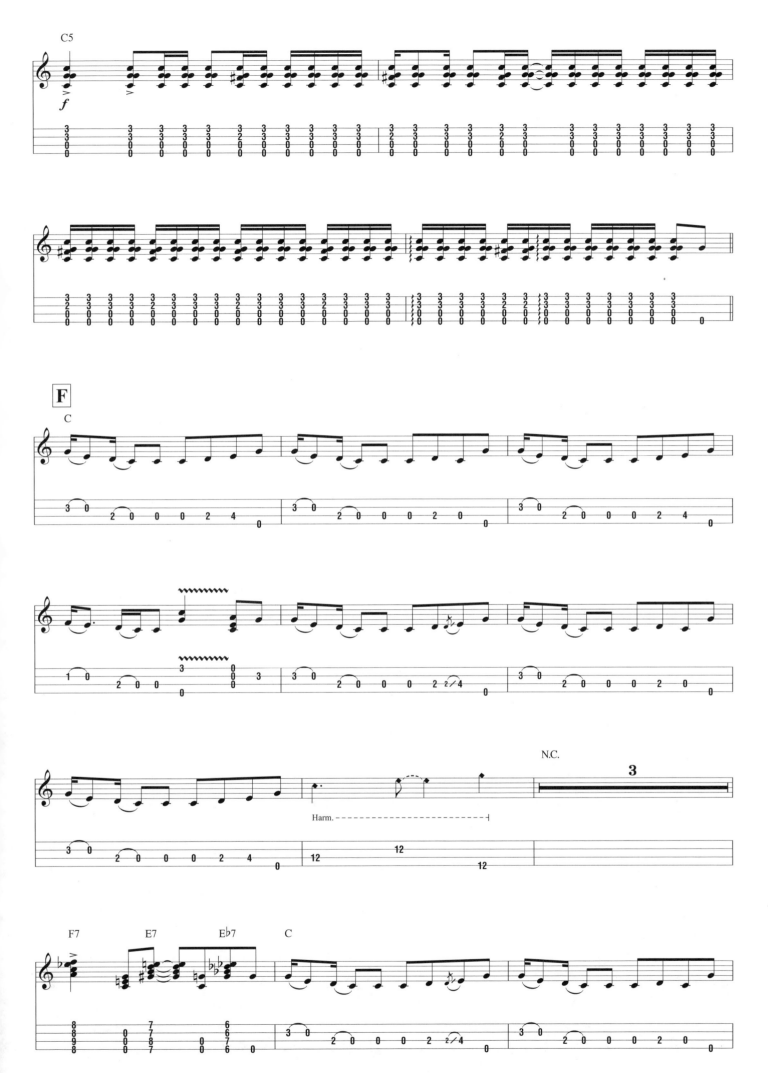

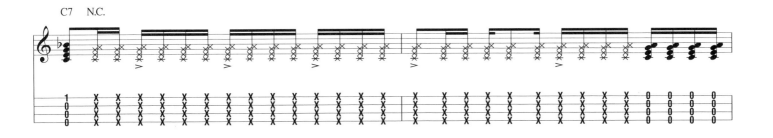

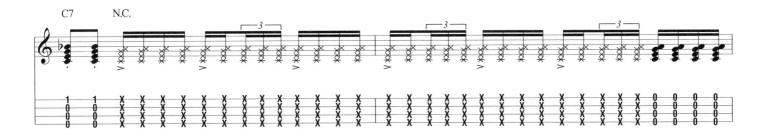

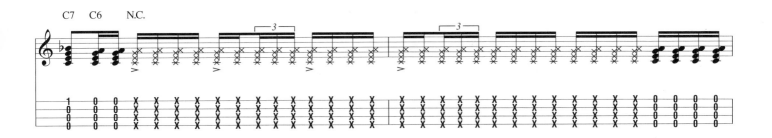

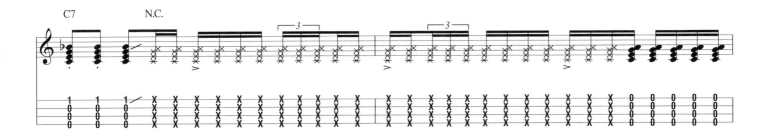

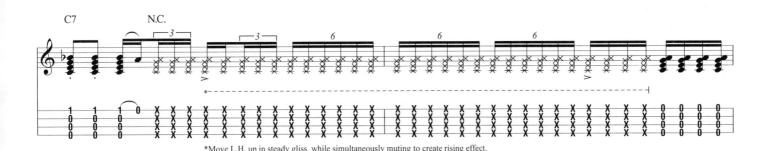

*Move L.H. up in steady gliss. while simultaneously muting to create rising effect.

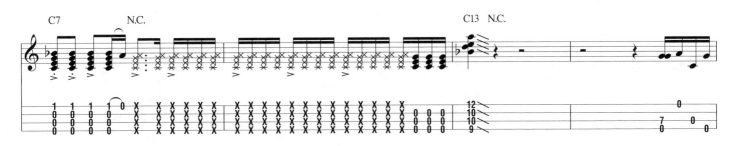

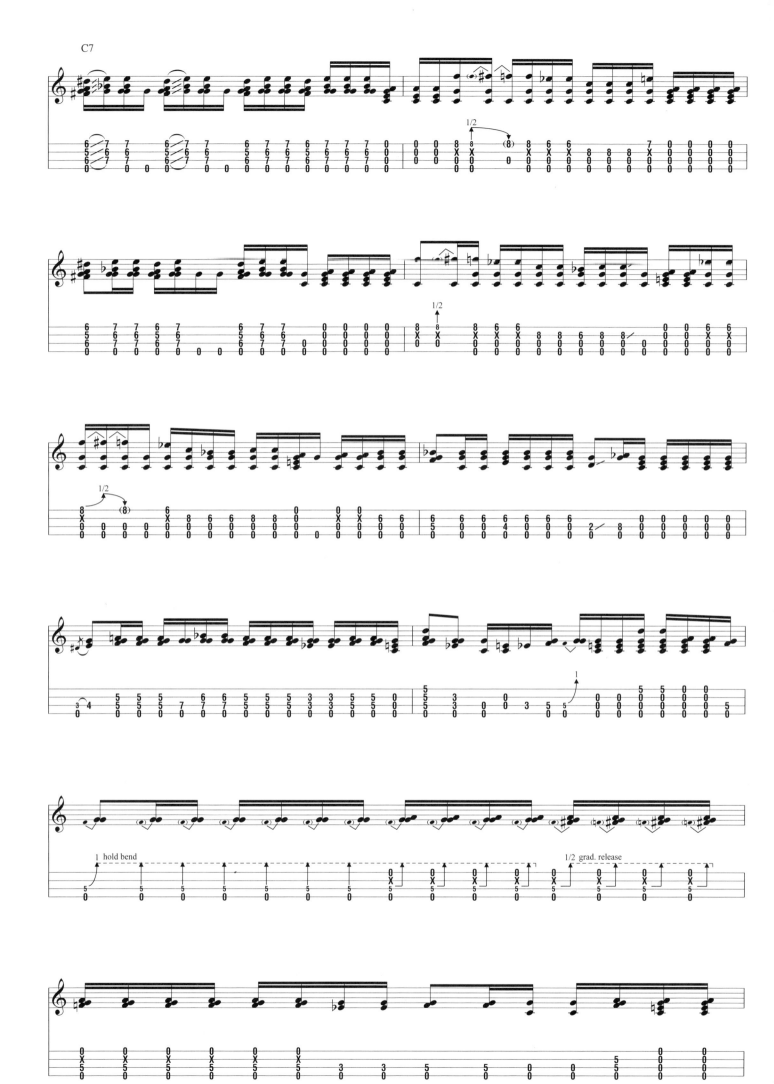

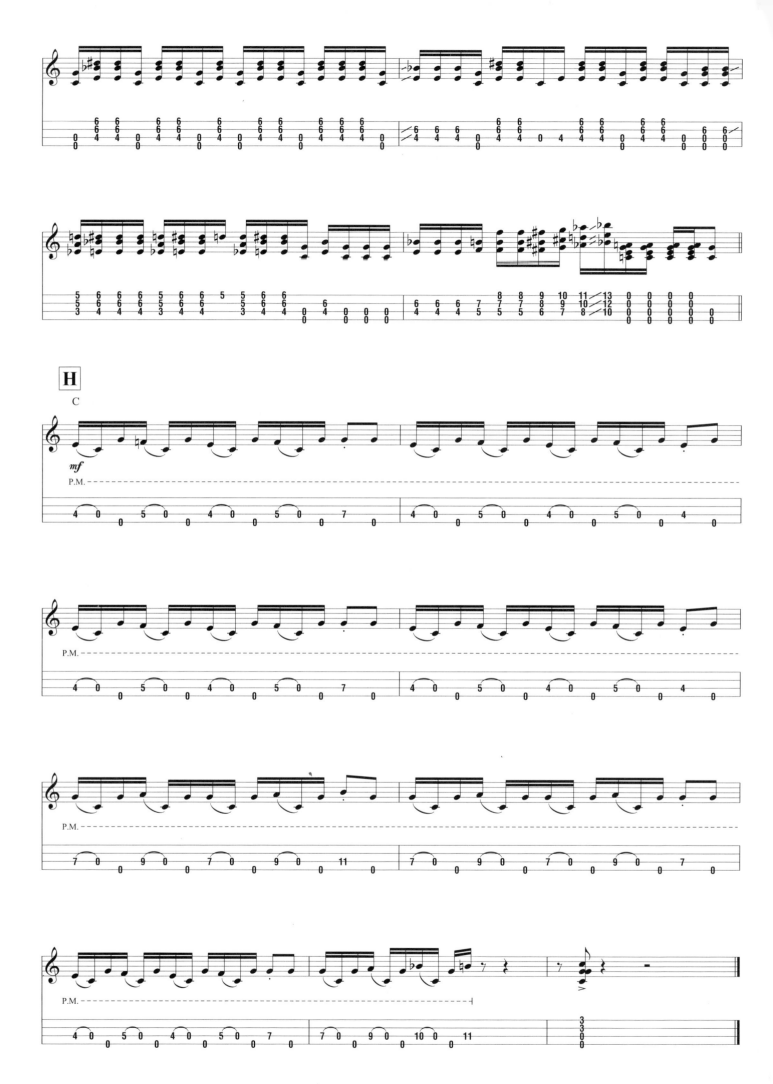

While My Guitar Gently Weeps

Words and Music by George Harrison

*Chord symbols reflect implied harmony.

Copyright © 1968 Harrisongs Ltd.
Copyright Renewed 1997
All Rights Reserved

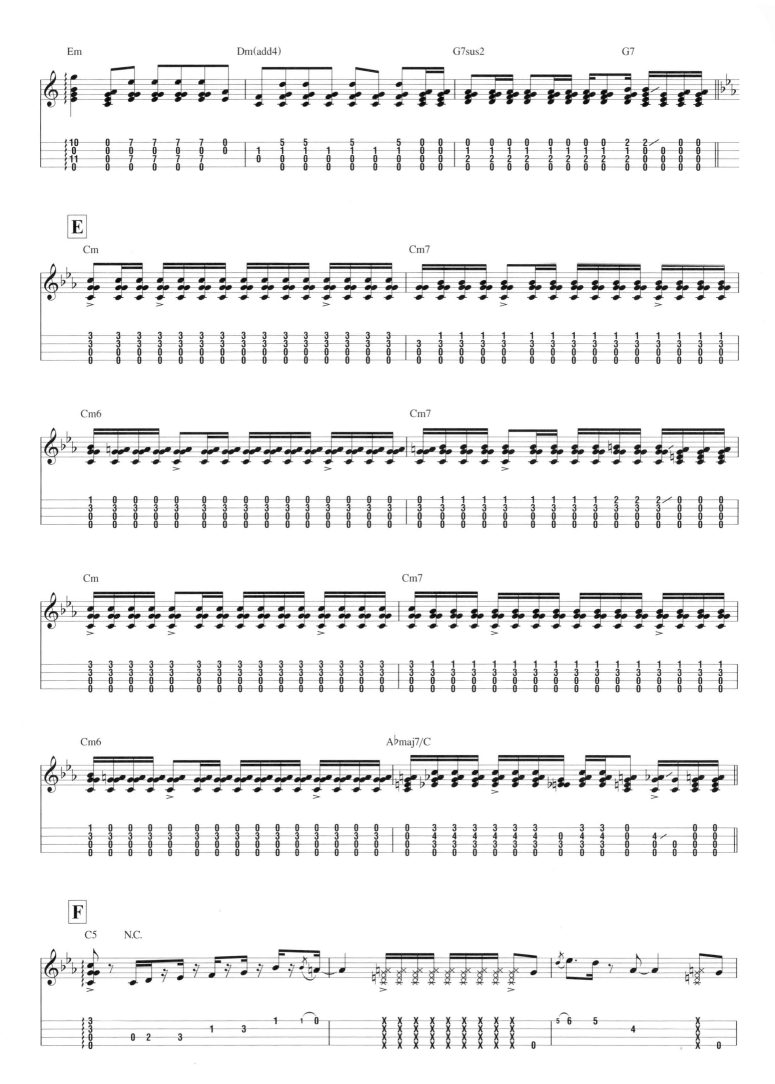

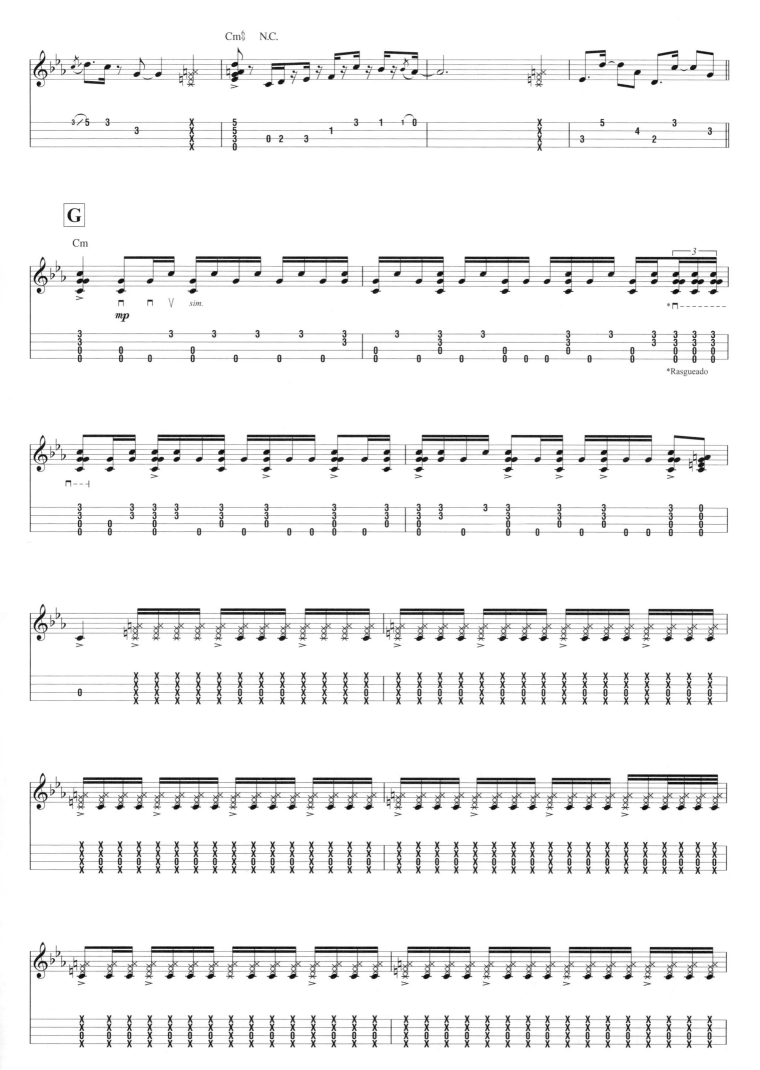

*Rasgueado

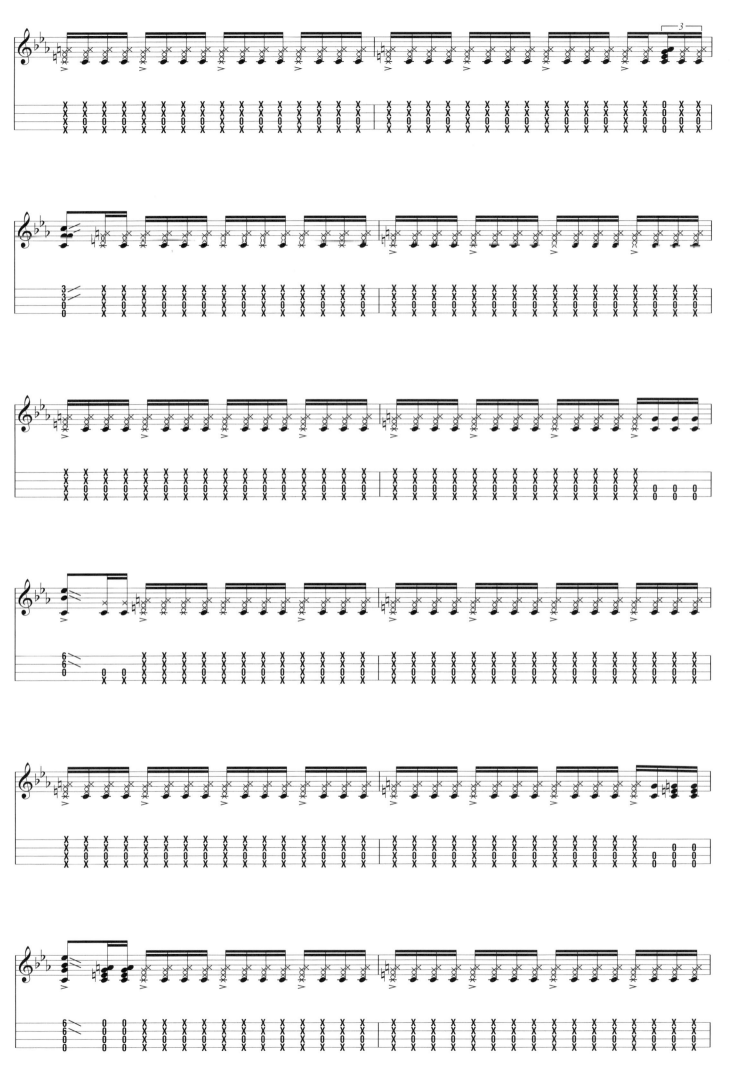

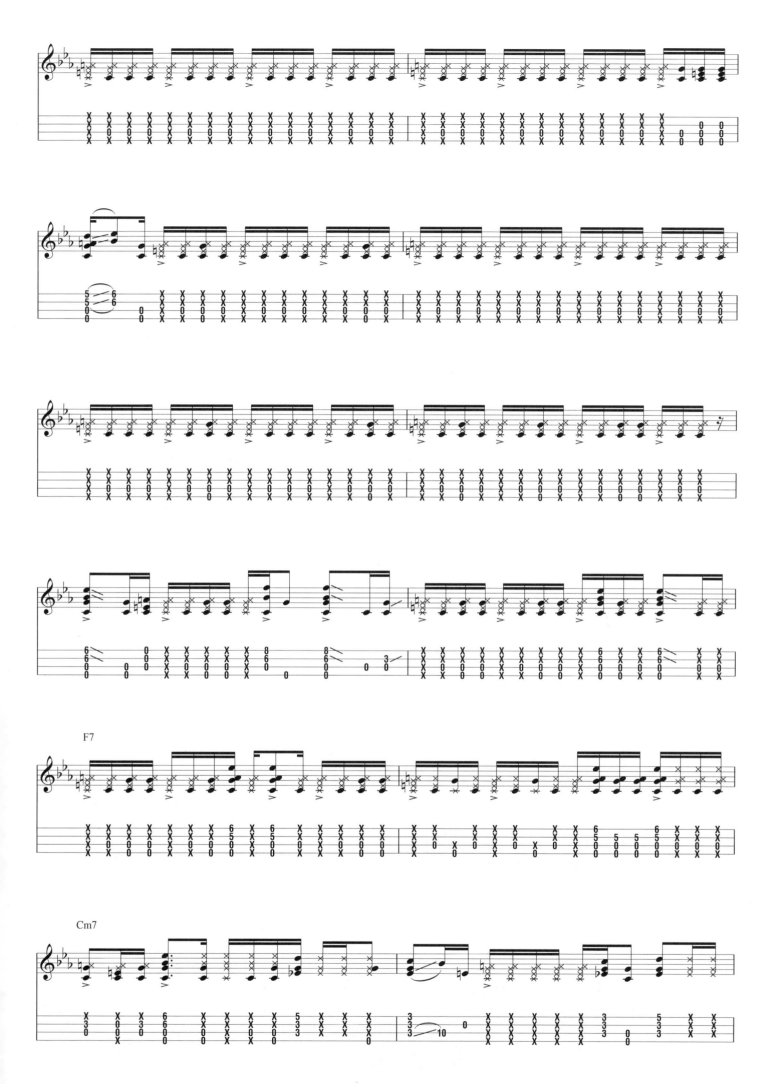

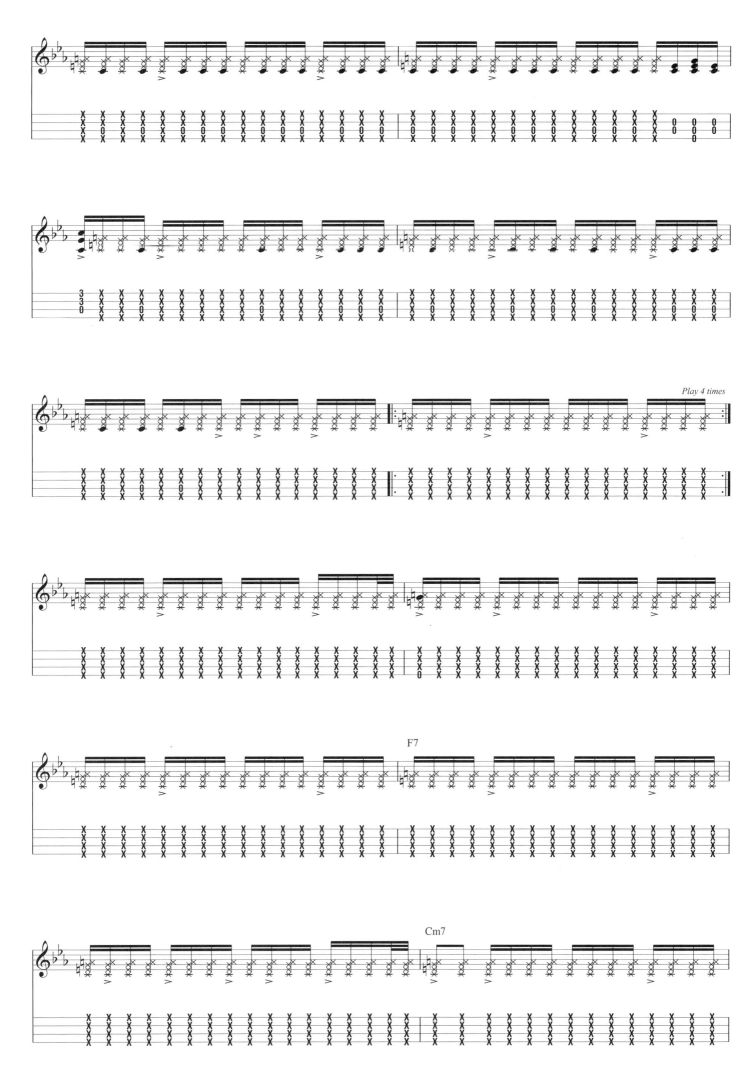

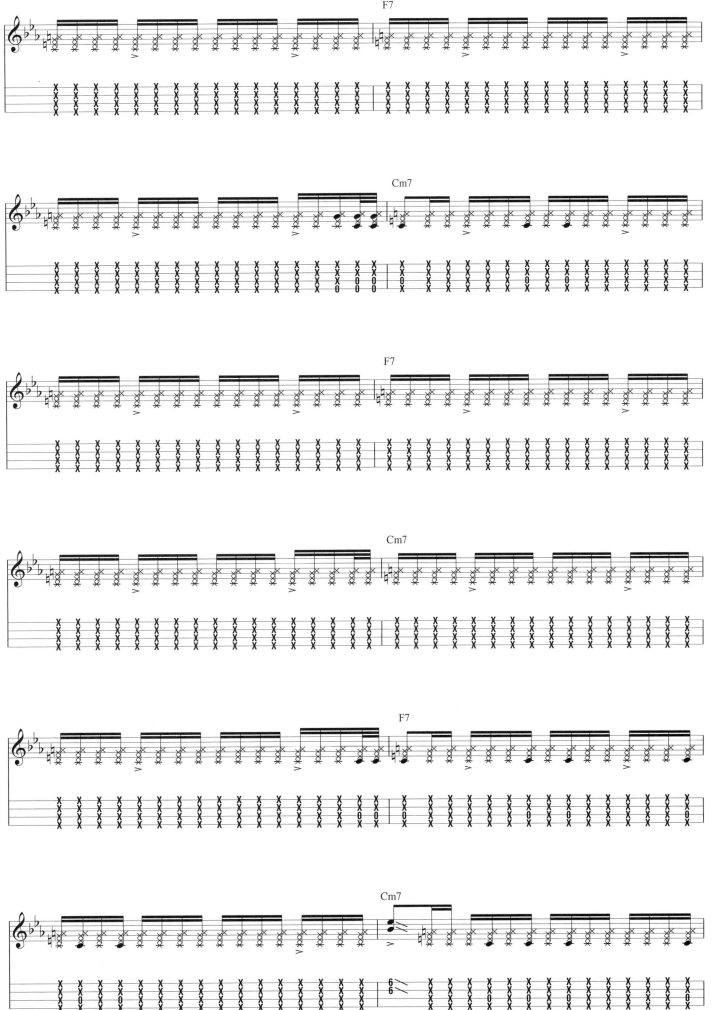

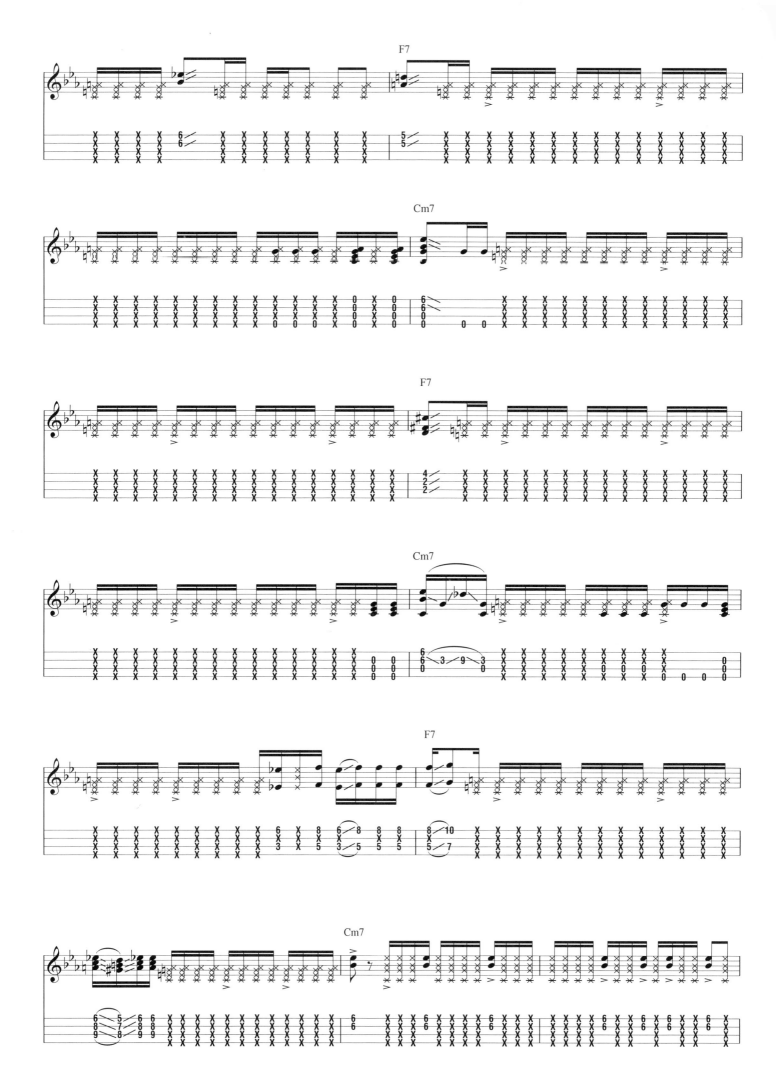

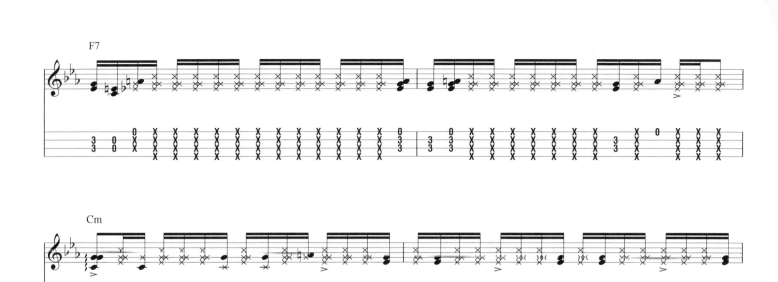

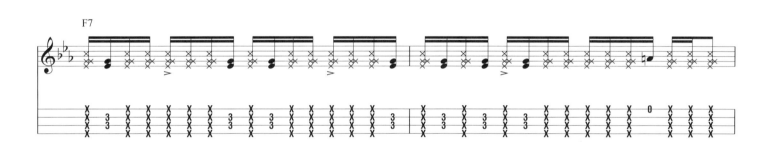

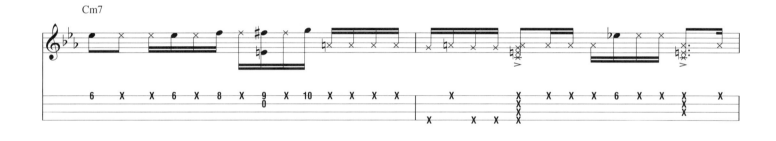

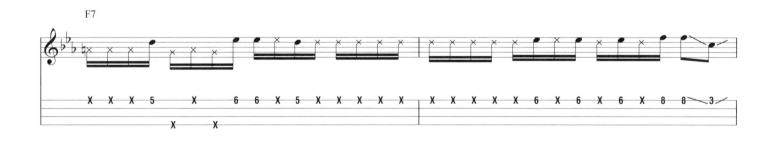

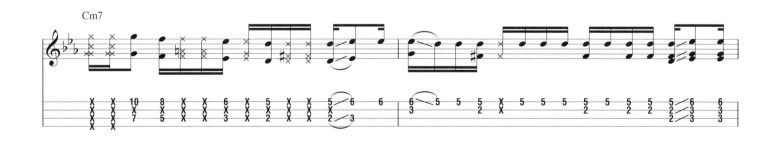

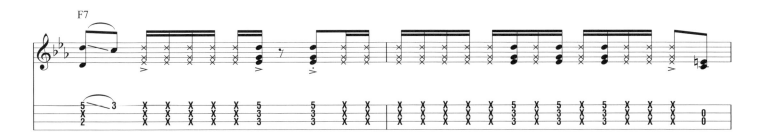

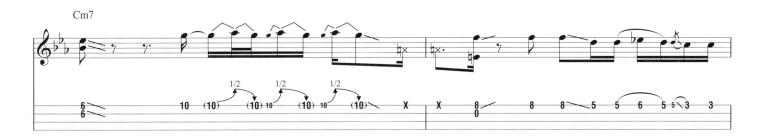

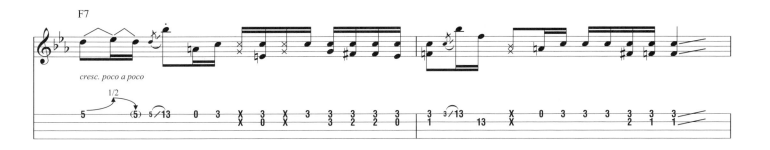

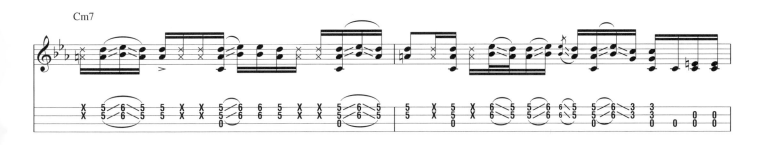

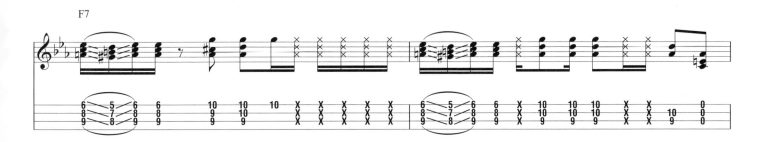

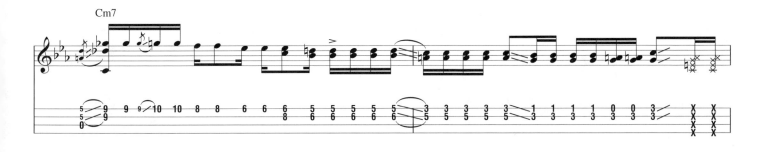

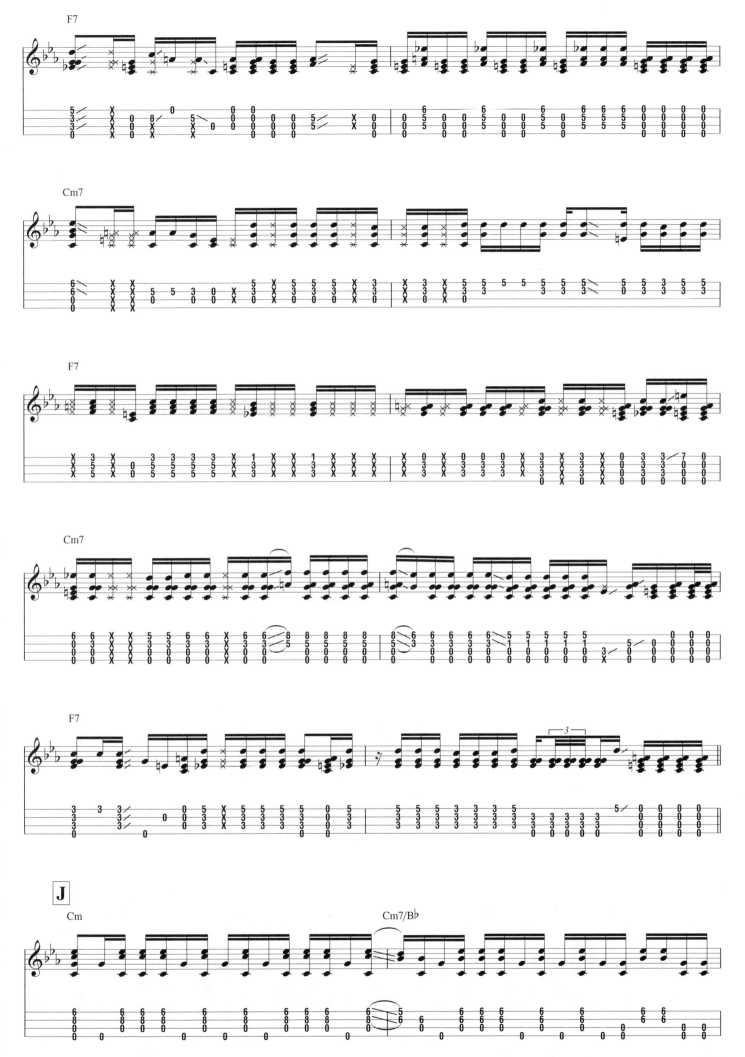

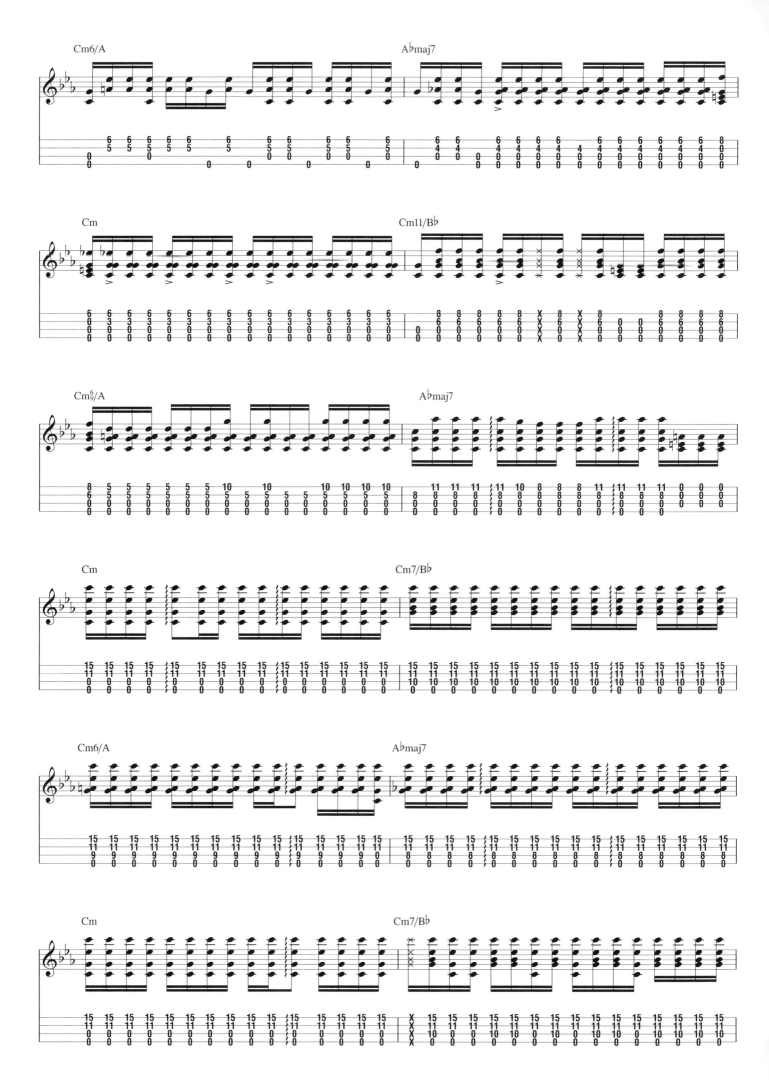

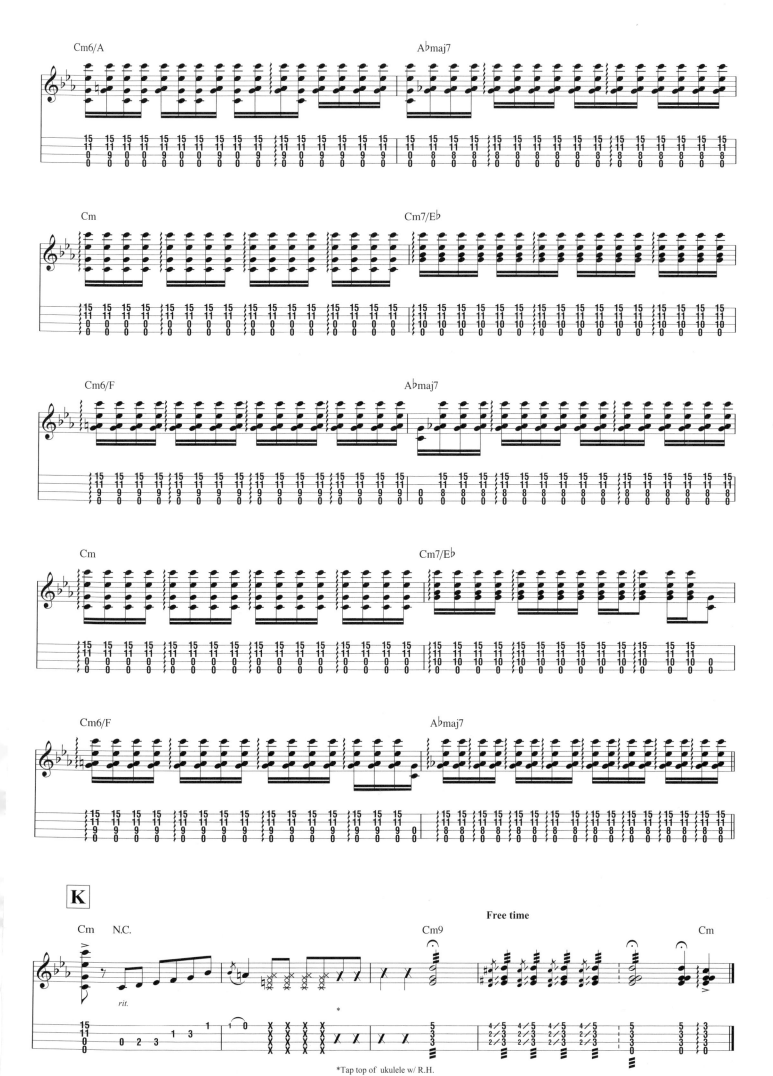

UKULELE NOTATION LEGEND

THE MUSICAL STAFF shows pitches and rhythms and is divided by bar lines into measures. Pitches are named after the first seven letters of the alphabet.

TABLATURE graphically represents the ukulele fingerboard. Each horizontal line represents a a string, and each number represents a fret.

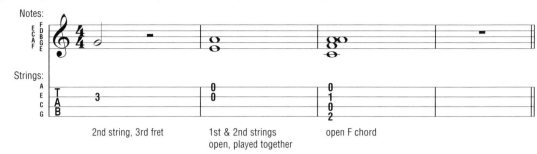

2nd string, 3rd fret   1st & 2nd strings open, played together   open F chord

HALF-STEP BEND: Strike the note and bend up 1/2 step.

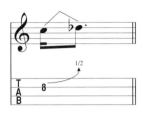

WHOLE-STEP BEND: Strike the note and bend up one step.

GRACE NOTE BEND: Strike the note and immediately bend up as indicated.

SLIGHT (MICROTONE) BEND: Strike the note and bend up 1/4 step.

BEND AND RELEASE: Strike the note and bend up as indicated, then release back to the original note. Only the first note is struck.

PRE-BEND: Bend the note as indicated, then strike it.

VIBRATO: The string is vibrated by rapidly bending and releasing the note with the fretting hand.

HAMMER-ON: Strike the first (lower) note with one finger, then sound the higher note (on the same string) with another finger by fretting it without picking.

PULL-OFF: Place both fingers on the notes to be sounded. Strike the first note and without picking, pull the finger off to sound the second (lower) note.

LEGATO SLIDE: Strike the first note and then slide the same fret-hand finger up or down to the second note. The second note is not struck.

SHIFT SLIDE: Same as legato slide, except the second note is struck.

TRILL: Very rapidly alternate between the notes indicated by continuously hammering on and pulling off.

TREMOLO PICKING: The note is picked as rapidly and continuously as possible.

NOTE: Tablature numbers in parentheses mean:

1. The note is being sustained over a system (note in standard notation is tied), or

2. The note is sustained, but a new articulation (such as a hammer-on, pull-off, slide or vibrato) begins, or

3. The note is a barely audible "ghost" note (note in standard notation is also in parentheses).

Additional Musical Definitions

 *(accent)* • Accentuate note (play it louder)

 *(staccato)* • Play the note short

D.S. al Coda • Go back to the sign (𝄋), then play until the measure marked "***To Coda***," then skip to the section labelled "**Coda**."

D.C. al Fine • Go back to the beginning of the song and play until the measure marked "***Fine***" (end).

N.C. • No chord.

 • Repeat measures between signs.

 • When a repeated section has different endings, play the first ending only the first time and the second ending only the second time.